S. Hrg. 112–623

CLEAN ENERGY RACE: THE UNITED STATES AND CHINA

HEARING

BEFORE THE

COMMITTEE ON ENERGY AND NATURAL RESOURCES UNITED STATES SENATE

ONE HUNDRED TWELFTH CONGRESS

SECOND SESSION

TO

RECEIVE TESTIMONY ON COMPETITIVENESS AND COLLABORATION
BETWEEN THE U.S. AND CHINA ON CLEAN ENERGY

JUNE 14, 2012

Printed for the use of the
Committee on Energy and Natural Resources

U.S. GOVERNMENT PRINTING OFFICE

76–898 PDF   WASHINGTON : 2012

For sale by the Superintendent of Documents, U.S. Government Printing Office
Internet: bookstore.gpo.gov   Phone: toll free (866) 512–1800; DC area (202) 512–1800
Fax: (202) 512–2104   Mail: Stop IDCC, Washington, DC 20402–0001

CONTENTS

STATEMENTS

APPENDIX

CLEAN ENERGY RACE: THE UNITED STATES AND CHINA

THURSDAY, JUNE 14, 2012

U.S. SENATE,
COMMITTEE ON ENERGY AND NATURAL RESOURCES,
Washington, DC.

The committee met, pursuant to notice, at 9:36 a.m. in room SD–366, Dirksen Senate Office Building, Hon. Jeff Bingaman, chairman, presiding.

OPENING STATEMENT OF HON. JEFF BINGAMAN, U.S. SENATOR FROM NEW MEXICO

The CHAIRMAN. I'm told Senator Murkowski is on her way and said we should proceed. Today we'll hear from witnesses on competitiveness and collaboration issues between the United States and China related to clean energy. The hearing follows a trip that I took to China in April to try to learn about Chinese policies and incentives to deploy clean energy. My staff and I visited Hong Kong and Shenzhen and Beijing to talk with investors and business representatives and government officials.

On that trip I was impressed by the vast combination of financial investments and government partnerships with industry to deploy clean energy. China is rapidly developing and, although much of its growth is dominated by coal and fossil fuels, the Chinese government has combined a mix of financial incentives with government policies to promote the clean energy sector as well.

That sector is not only developing domestically in China; it's also extending abroad. It's influencing the United States very directly and European markets.

The situation in China is in direct contrast to the approach to clean energy that we have taken here in the United States. Many of our efforts to promote clean tech in the United States are addressed in an unpredictable fashion, with funds and incentives that expire and come back to life and expire again, and a lack of clear directional policy that would allow industry to plan for the future.

I believe that the inconsistent approach that we've been pursuing has put the United States at a disadvantage in competing with China for a share of clean energy markets, both at home and abroad. Many here in the United States argue that we should allow the free market to determine the fate of domestic industries. There's clearly truth in that suggestion, but it fails to take into account the industrial policies and practices of competing nations, as well as hidden costs in the current energy system.

(1)

The U.S. cannot compete on a level playing field with countries that have strong industrial policies when our own policies are inconsistent and erratic. In the absence of clear and coherent policies to support development of clean technology in the United States, many of our companies and industries are left to rely on trade policy to try to protect their competitive interests. Trade enforcement is critical, but we also need a strong foundation of domestic policies to build upon.

I want to make clear that this is not a hearing intended to focus on the trade cases that are currently before the ITC and the Department of Commerce. The matters in these cases are not under the jurisdiction of our committee. This hearing should not be a forum to try to prejudice the outcome of any of those cases. The purpose of this hearing is to gain a greater understanding of what China's doing on clean energy, how that impacts and relates to what the U.S. is doing.

I hope we're able to focus on 3 large issues: What's the current landscape of Chinese investment in clean and renewable energy; second, what are the appropriate U.S.-Chinese relationships on clean energy issues; and how do we promote U.S. knowledge competitiveness with China and other countries in the clean tech sector.

I believe the U.S. should continue to rigorously enforce its trade laws to level the playing field when there are unfair disparities. But additional domestic measures are likely to be needed if the U.S. is to fully compete in this sector.

I'm very interested in some of the testimony related to the experience we had with Sematech back in the 1980s and drawing the analogy between what the United States did there to try to support the semiconductor industry and what might be done here with these clean technology areas that we're discussing today. I know Alan Wolff and Clyde Prestowitz have a substantial history in connection with this and may be able to enlighten us as well.

Finally, the U.S. and China have common interests in deploying clean energy. While we may find ourselves. While we may find ourselves in positions of competing with each other for these new markets, I believe that part of our conversation should also lead to answers on what the two countries can be doing together to accelerate deployment of these technologies.

Let me call on Senator Murkowski for any comments she would like to make.

STATEMENT OF HON. LISA MURKOWSKI, U.S. SENATOR FROM ALASKA

Senator MURKOWSKI. Thank you, Mr. Chairman. To the witnesses, welcome and good morning.

The purpose of today's hearing is to take another, perhaps a closer, look at clean tech competitiveness issues between China and the United States. I want to reinforce the chairman's remarks here that this hearing is not about ongoing trade disputes. It's not the role of this committee to influence those processes. Focusing, I think, in other topics will not diminish our conversation, but rather, to the contrary, competitiveness challenges surface long before trade complaints are filed. They emerge even before the goods are manufactured or the factories are built, because they start with the decisions made by companies and individuals about where to invest.

The factors guiding these decisions are nearly limitless and they are no different when the choice is between the United States and China or any other country. Regulatory and tax treatments, property rights, raw material availability, labor, health care costs, access to affordable energy, all of these combine to guide investment decisions.

Our work to better understand these forces can benefit from comparisons with China, but there are also some key differences that I think it's important that we keep in mind. These differences are rooted in some very important factors, including what our own Constitution permits, how much taxpayer we can afford to spend, what the American people really are willing to support.

I'm one who believes that we need to be mindful of these factors when we hear claims that the United States is somehow falling behind China in a clean energy race. In so many ways, I would suggest that we are not falling behind. From the wages and conditions for our workers to our environmental standards and capacity for innovation, I think that the United States is leading.

We can and should work with China to make progress on our energy challenges, but we should not necessarily copy what they do or how they do it just for the sake of copying what they do. Imitating China is not the best way to compete with China. This is particularly true for energy technology subsidies as we work to get our debt under control. I have long advocated for funding clean tech research efforts with revenues from conventional energy sources. This I think is a far more sustainable approach than the one taken by China. I hope that we continue to gain in traction in that direction.

Beyond spending, I think we need to be careful about following even China's more progressive energy policy. An example would be the Three Gorges Dam, a source of renewable energy, but it has displaced several million people from their homes and their communities. Chinese production of raw materials for clean energy technologies has had some negative impacts on their country's air and water quality. The solar panel factories don't necessarily run on solar power.

But, having said all that, I think we also recognize that our country policies are not perfect, either. Even here at home, where we've got a proud history of improving environmental performance, biofuels have played a role in raising our food prices. We currently have no plan for permanent disposal of our spent nuclear fuel and nuclear waste. The siting of transmission lines to connect renewable assets to the grid has, of course, resulted in some controversy out there.

I raise these issues, not to throw cold water on the enthusiasm for clean energy technologies, but perhaps to provide some context and a reminder to us of the challenges that we face. It's my hope that this hearing serves as the basis for understanding how cautious we must be about accepting some of the simple narratives.

In the end, this is not just about lowering the cost of financing projects that we all support or finding the money in the budget for subsidies. It's about looking honestly at the whole picture, devoting as much attention to identifying areas where our own government can play a constructive role as we do identifying areas where it's getting in the way. It's about balancing the priorities and reaching agreement on the policies that address both our immediate and our long-term needs.

The discussion must account for China, but I don't think that we should be overwhelmed by it.

I appreciate the fact that we have the opportunity to have this hearing this morning, Mr. Chairman. I look forward to the statements and comments from the witnesses.

The CHAIRMAN. Thank you very much.

We have 5 distinguished witnesses here and let me just introduce all of them, and then we'll hearing from them: Mr. Justin Wu, who is head of wind industry research with Bloomberg New Energy Finance in Hong Kong. We appreciate you being here very much.

Mr. Alan Wolff, who is Senior Counsel with McKenna Long and Aldridge, we appreciate you being here very much.

Mr. Clyde Prestowitz, who's testified many times before our committee, as have some of the other witnesses, President of the Economic Strategy Institute, we appreciate you being here.

Mr. Dan Holladay, Director of Advanced technologies and PV Programs with Sematech, thank you.

Dr. Derek Scissors, who is the Senior Research Fellow at the Heritage Foundation, thank you for being here.

Our usual approach is to take—have each witness take 5 or 6 minutes and summarize the main points that you think we should understand from your testimony. We will include your full testimony in the record as if read, but if you could try to give us the main points, that way we will have some time for questions.

So why don't we just go in the order I introduced people. Mr. Wu, why don't you start.

STATEMENT OF JUSTIN WU, HEAD OF WIND INDUSTRY RESEARCH, BLOOMBERG NEW ENERGY FINANCE

Mr. WU. Thank you very much. Good morning, Chairman Bingaman, Senators, ladies and gentlemen: Thank you very much for hosting me here today. It is an honor and privilege to be offering my thoughts on these important topics before this committee.

I join you in my role as an analyst with Bloomberg New Energy Finance, a division of Bloomberg focused on the clean energy sector. Our group provides accurate and actionable data and insight on investment, technology, and policy trends in clean energy. My remarks today represent my views alone and not the corporate positions of either Bloomberg or Bloomberg New Energy Finance. In addition, they do not represent any investment advice and should not be construed as such.

The subject of today's hearing is China, clean energy and the trade relationship between the United States and China. I grew up in Maryland and have worked in China and Hong Kong over the past 6 years analyzing the growth of China's clean energy industry. I offer my thoughts on its current status and how it has developed so rapidly and what we can expect in the future. I will leave to my fellow panelists today to discuss more specifically the relevant trade and cooperation issues.

There is no question that China is now a clean energy giant. Its industry has grown rapidly from almost nothing in less than a decade. The country now manufactures half the world's wind turbines and solar PV modules. Four of the ten largest wind turbine manufacturers and 8 of the top ten solar manufacturers in the world are Chinese. The country overtook the United States as the world's largest wind market in 2010 and installed more than 10,000 wind turbines in 2011. That represents almost ten times the capacity of the Hoover Dam.

In 2009 and 2010 China was the world leader in attracting new capital for clean energy. In 2011, a total of $47 billion went into the country's wind, solar, and other clean energy sectors, though China actually finished second to the United States last year in total clean energy investment, for reasons which I will explain in a moment.

What has driven this massive growth? First, the Chinese economy is expanding at about 8 percent per year, with electricity demand growth to match. Its utilities and power generators have to invest heavily in new capacity to keep pace.

Second, over 70 percent of China's electricity currently comes from coal. In the view of the Chinese government, this overreliance has become expensive, environmentally damaging, and bad for energy security. The need to diversify into something cleaner and less vulnerable to fuel price shock is attractive and important.

In 2005, the Chinese government drafted its first renewable energy law, which set targets for non-large hydro renewable energy and mandated that its utilities procure a certain portion of electricity from these clean sources. This was followed by other supportive measures, including feed-in tariffs, which set high prices for power sold from wind or biomass projects, and laws that required grid companies to prioritize dispatch of renewables.

A vision for renewables was outlined at the national level and China's state-owned utilities and industry embraced these goals. Local governments followed, offering land and tax incentives to clean energy companies to set up shop in their home provinces. State-owned banks lent generously to power companies to build their wind farms and solar parks.

A domestic clean energy manufacturing industry was built alongside the generation capacity. Chinese state-owned corporations, many with previous heavy manufacturing or construction experience, began buying technology licenses, forming joint ventures, and hiring foreign engineers to design their wind turbines. Private entrepreneurs, some backed by venture capital and private equity money from abroad, began building solar manufacturing facilities. The ultimate result, a manufacturing boom and the creation of leading clean energy companies.

It should be noted that a number of European and American clean tech companies have also benefited from this boom. Advanced components of wind turbines were designed and supplied by European firms and capital equipment used to manufacture solar cells and modules often comes from American companies.

However, China's clean energy boom is not without its problems. The rapid growth of the industry has created a clean energy bubble. There are far too many wind and solar manufacturing companies and many now face intense competitive pressure and possible bankruptcy. One-quarter of China's wind farms are not connected to the power grid.

They sit idle in remote regions with poor infrastructure and very little electricity demand.

Today, China's clean energy industry is still growing, but this growth has moderated significantly and a more mature industry will eventually emerge. The government is trying to cool investment in this sector and reduce the number of new wind farms and solar parks being built in the country each year to a more sustainable level. The focus is now more on quality and not on quantity.

This change, coupled with major U.S. Government support in the form of stimulus programs, allowed the U.S. to regain its leadership position in clean energy investment dollars in 2011. That said, we regard it as unlikely that the U.S. will top the table again in 2012, as policy uncertainty appears to be depressing investment, particularly in the wind sector.

Finally, I would like to address the question of what's next for Chinese clean energy companies. As the industry cools at home, many are now seeking opportunities abroad. China has a surplus of savings and a strong need for further investment to drive its economic growth, including more investment overseas. Its government has encouraged the clean energy industry to do this.

Chinese solar companies have exported their equipment to Germany, the United States, and elsewhere for years. But Chinese wind turbine manufacturers, utilities, and other clean tech investors have remained largely confined to the domestic market. In the coming months, we anticipate Chinese power companies and banks developing and financing clean energy projects abroad, not only in the United States, but also in Europe and emerging markets, particularly in Latin America.

At the same time, American and European clean energy companies will continue to sell their products and technology to China and also partner with Chinese companies as they go overseas. The trade flow in clean energy between the United States and China will only increase in the future and it will be a two-way street. However, unlike the breakneck pace of Chinese domestic clean energy investment, overseas wind ventures have so far been slow and cautious, a trickle and not a flood.

Thank you for your time and attention. I welcome your questions and comments.

[The prepared statement of Mr. Wu follows:]

PREPARED STATEMENT OF JUSTIN WU, HEAD OF WIND INDUSTRY RESEARCH, BLOOMBERG NEW ENERGY FINANCE

Good morning, Chairman Bingaman, Senators, ladies and gentlemen. Thank you very much for hosting me here today. It is an honor and privilege to be offering my thoughts on these important topics before this committee.

I join you in my role as analyst with Bloomberg New Energy Finance, a division of Bloomberg focused on the clean energy sector. Our group provides accurate and actionable data and insight on investment, technology, and policy trends in clean energy. My remarks today represent my views alone and not the corporate positions of either Bloomberg LP or Bloomberg New Energy Finance. In addition, they do not represent investment advice and should not be construed as such.

The subject of today's hearing is China, clean energy and the trade relationship between the United States and China in this area. I grew up in Maryland and have worked in China and Hong Kong over the past six years analyzing the growth of China's clean energy industry. I offer my thoughts on its current status, how it has developed so rapidly and what we can expect in the future. I will leave to my fellow panelists today to discuss more specifically the relevant trade and cooperation issues.

There is no question that China is now a clean energy giant—its industry has grown rapidly from almost nothing in less than a decade. The country now manufactures half the world's wind turbines and solar PV modules. Four of the 10 largest wind turbine manufacturers and eight of the top ten solar manufacturers in the world are Chinese.

The country overtook the United States as the world's largest wind market in 2010 and installed more than 10,000 wind turbines in 2011. That represents almost ten times the capacity of the Hoover Dam.

In 2009 and 2010, China was the world leader in attracting new capital for clean energy. In 2011, a total of $47bn went into the country's wind, solar, and other clean energy sectors, though China actually finished second to the US last year in total clean energy investment for reasons I'll explain in just a moment.

What has driven this massive growth? First, the Chinese economy is expanding at about 8% per year with electricity demand growth to match. Its utilities and power generators have to invest heavily in new capacity to keep pace. Second, over 70% of China's electricity comes from coal. In the view of the Chinese government, this over reliance has become expensive, environmentally damaging and bad for energy security. The need to diversify into something cleaner and less vulnerable to fuel price shock is attractive and important.

In 2005, the Chinese government drafted its first Renewable Energy Law which set targets for non-large hydro renewable energy and mandated that its utilities procure a certain portion of electricity from clean sources. This was followed by other supportive measures including feed-in tariffs, which set fixed high prices for power sold from wind or biomass projects, and laws that require grid companies to prioritize dispatch of renewables.

A vision for renewables was outlined at the national level and China's state-owned utilities and industry embraced these goals. Local governments followed, offering land and tax incentives to clean energy companies to set up shop in their home provinces. State-owned banks lent generously to power companies to build their wind farms and solar parks.

A domestic clean energy manufacturing industry was built alongside the generation capacity. Chinese state-owned corporations, many with previous heavy manufacturing or construction experience began buying technology licenses, forming joint ventures and hiring foreign engineers to design their wind turbines. Private entrepreneurs, some backed by venture capital and private equity money from abroad, began building solar manufacturing facilities. The ultimate result: a manufacturing boom and the creation of leading clean energy companies.

It should be noted that a number of European and American clean tech companies have also benefited from this boom. Advanced components of wind turbines were designed and supplied by European firms, and capital equipment used to manufacture solar cells and modules often comes from American companies.

However, China's clean energy boom is not without its problems. The rapid growth of the industry has created a clean energy bubble—there are far too many wind and solar manufacturing companies and many now face intense competitive pressure and possible bankruptcy. One quarter of China's wind farms are not connected to the power grid; they sit idle in remote regions with poor infrastructure and very little electricity demand.

Today China's clean energy industry is still growing, but this growth has moderated significantly and a more mature industry will eventually emerge. The government is trying to cool investment in this sector and reduce the number of new wind farms and solar parks being built in the country each year to a more sustainable level. The focus is more on quality than quantity.

This change, coupled with major US government support in the form of stimulus programs, allowed the US to regain its leadership position in clean energy investment in 2011. That said, we regard it as unlikely that the US will top the table again in 2012 as policy uncertainty appears to be depressing investment, particularly in the wind sector.

Finally, I would like to address the question of what's next for Chinese clean energy companies. As the industry cools at home, many are now seeking opportunities abroad. China has a surplus of savings and a strong need for further investment to drive its economic growth, including more investment overseas. Its government has encouraged the clean energy industry to do this.

Chinese solar companies have exported their equipment to Germany, the US, and elsewhere for years. But Chinese wind turbine manufacturers, utilities and other clean tech investors have remained largely confined to the domestic market. In coming months, we anticipate Chinese power companies and banks developing and financing clean energy projects abroad, not only the US, but in Europe and particularly in emerging markets such as Latin America.

At the same time, American and European clean energy companies will continue to sell their products and technology to China and also partner with Chinese companies as they go overseas. The trade flow in clean technology between the United States and China will only increase in the future—and it will be a two way street.

However, unlike the breakneck place of Chinese domestic clean energy investment, overseas ventures have so far been slow and cautious—a trickle and not a flood.

Thank you for your time and attention, I welcome your questions and comments.

The CHAIRMAN. Thank you very much.

Mr. Wolff, go right ahead.

STATEMENT OF ALAN WM. WOLFF, MCKENNA LONG AND ALDRIDGE

Mr. WOLFF. Thank you, Mr. Chairman, Senator Murkowski, Senators Wyden and Frank, and members of the committee.

Your hearing today on China and clean energy is both timely and important. China is out-investing the United States and that does have consequences in our market in clean energies. Their industrial policies have created tremendous excess capacity, particularly in photovoltaics.

China has exported until recently about 95 percent of its production in photovoltaics and it's now estimated to be around 75 percent.

Many U.S. PV producers are in serious economic trouble, in substantial part as a result of China's industrial policies. China has also shut its market to our wind turbine exports, as well as those of Europe and India.

U.S. measures, as you've pointed out, Mr. Chairman, in support of the industry are temporary, they're erratic, they're expiring. Confrontation over trade is likely within a few months with the U.S. antidumping case on solar and China's potential claim against U.S. State programs, as well as bringing its own—potentially bringing its own antidumping case on U.S. polysilicon.

Drawing on several experiences I have had, one is doing a study for the national—chair a committee at the National Academy of Science on comparative innovation policies, drawing on the time I've spent advising the U.S. semiconductor industry since 1980 in our problems with Japan, and the study* I did, co-authored, for the National Foreign Trade Council on China's support of renewable energy electric generating equipment, which I ask be entered in the record—it's not all that long.

The CHAIRMAN. We're glad to enter that in the record.

Thank you very much.

Mr. WOLFF. The questions I see before us are: Can we reach a national consensus that it's vitally important that clean energy account for a much greater supply of our total energy usage? Is com-

---

* Document has been retained in committee files.

plete U.S. domestic industrial production in the entire supply chain delivering clean energy efficiently from the production of photovoltaics through fabrication into panels and deployment on wind farms of vital importance to the U.S. economy? Decisions that have to be made.

As Senator Murkowski said, we're living in a time of fiscal constraint and these are difficult questions. But I would say there are two other questions that we have to face, and that is: Is it acceptable for Chinese industrial policy to shape the U.S. economy? I would suggest that it's not acceptable. Can the country afford not to seek to find which clean energy technologies lie just beyond the horizon? I think we have to.

So what should we do? We need a broad cross-sectoral set of measures, beyond the scope of this hearing, but in terms of taxation and job training, manufacturing, extension services, things that will boost our economy and job creation broadly, which are subjects the National Academy's report goes to.

For renewables, until costs come down there have to be mandates and subsidies if we're going to increase our deployment of clean energy and our production of the equipment that generates it.

I think we can learn some useful lessons from the Sematech and semiconductor experience, and you have a witness here who will talk about what's being done today. But in the 1980s Japan had a closed market, it was dumping its semiconductors, selling below cost of production, generation after generation of semiconductor product. Vertically integrated Japanese producers were quite able to sustain that policy of selling below average cost of production, and the Silicon Valley startups—Intel, AMD, National—were really on the verge of extinction.

U.S. companies needed unencumbered access to foreign markets, we needed to open the Japanese market, they needed to improve their manufacturing skills, they needed to continue to attract capital, they needed to improve the protection of the intellectual property, they needed to make sure universities were training engineers with relevant skills, they needed tax policies that supported the need for R and D spending.

In short, they needed a complete strategy, not just a partial strategy of just a trade element. In fact, all of the elements were put into place, and the result today is U.S. semiconductors, which were half the world market share in the mid-1980s of Japan, are now double the Japanese market share. We're over half the world in terms of supplying global needs, and semiconductors account for one of the top 5 exports of the United States. There's major new facilities that have gone into upper New York State now with Global Foundries, and the years of turbulence are behind us. We're now very good friends with the Japanese producers and their government, working together on things like energy saving and reduction of use of harmful chemicals.

So what do we need now? We need to have market stability, predictability for both the Chinese and the U.S. producers. We need to—from the Chinese perspective, they probably need to avoid large deposits, cash deposits at the U.S. Treasury, if they are found to be dumping. There's room for mutual cooperation, enhanced mutual cooperation, in R and D, and potential Chinese investment in the U.S. market.

Ultimately, trade measures and domestic policies should be integrated into a strategic approach, as we did in semiconductors. Down the road, maybe we get the Europeans involved as well. They face some of the same concerns that we do.

The bottom line is I believe there is a negotiated solution out there. It probably won't come by October or November. But there are mutual interests that we should explore with China and reach, I would hope, an accommodation that doesn't end up in just a trade dispute that goes on for some years.

Thank you.

[The prepared statement of Mr. Wolff follows:]

PREPARED STATEMENT OF ALAN WM. WOLFF, MCKENNA LONG & ALDRIDGE

Mr. Chairman, members of the Committee, the subject of your hearing today concerns one of the most important challenges facing America today—our country's future in clean energy.

During 2011, fourteen solar energy companies announced plans to scale back or cease U.S. production, five were in bankruptcy or insolvency. Although the picture is mixed[1] a substantial number of others are in serious financial difficulties. In wind power, foreign wind turbine producers share of the Chinese market dropped from 75% in 2004 to 11% in 2010. See Chart 1. There are clear limits to the degree to which the U.S. market can be served with hydro power (even taking into account additional hydro power from Canada) and biofuels have not yet reached a stage where they can play a major role in the near-term expansion of electric power derived from renewables. Solar and wind must form an increasing part of the future source of U.S. energy needs, and the American industries producing the equipment needed to generate these forms of energy are under siege.

There are a number of causes of the current problem. The welcome discovery of large untapped volumes of commercially accessible natural gas has had and will continue to have a major near term depressing effect on the development of renewable energy even when a new equilibrium price for natural gas is established. But there is a second major factor affecting U.S. productive capacity in this sector that is less welcome, and that is the entry of China as a key producer of renewable energy equipment because its industrial policies are re-shaping an important segment of the U.S. economy. Global overcapacity, and particularly overcapacity in China in polysilicon PV manufacturing, is having a worldwide depressing effect on the PV manufacturing industry.[2] Market barriers to wind energy equipment are equally troubling.

I have spent the better part of my professional life analyzing and dealing with competitive challenges to U.S. industries. As trade counsel to the U.S. Semiconductor Industry Association (SIA), I was actively involved in the U.S. industry's efforts to survive and become fully competitive when Japanese industrial policy threatened to eliminate our industry. More recently, I have been actively engaged in the work of the Science Technology and Economic Policy (STEP) Board of the National Academies. I chair the Board's Committee on Comparative Innovation Policies, which will soon publish its final report entitled Rising to the Challenge: U.S. Innovation Policy for the Global Economy. I also chair the Board of the National Foreign Trade Council (NFTC) which published a study in 2010 that I co-authored entitled China's Promotion of the Renewable Electric Power Equipment Industry—Hydro, Wind, Solar, Biomass.[3] I am, however, appearing today in an individual capacity and not speaking for any client or institution.

You have posed three questions.

• What is the current landscape of Chinese investment in clean and renewable energy?
• How do we promote U.S. competitiveness with China in the clean tech sector?

[1] In March, 2012, Stion, a manufacturer of high-efficiency thin-film solar modules, began to ship modules produced at its Hattiesburg, Ms., factory.
* Charts 1 and 2 have been retained in committee files.
[2] Asian producers are as a result scaling back.
[3] http://www.nftc.org/default/Press%20Release/2010/China%20Renewable%20Energy.pdf

• What are the appropriate U.S.-Chinese relationships on clean energy?

In my oral remarks, I will, as you have requested, concentrate on addressing questions #2 and #3.

THE CURRENT LANDSCAPE OF CHINESE INVESTMENT IN CLEAN AND RENEWABLE ENERGY

China leads the world in installed clean energy capacity as of 2011[4]. See Table 1 and Chart 2. This is the result of many years of government mandates and subsidies. The 2002 Government Procurement Law required government entities to purchase domestic products, which was one spur to China's development of the equipment needed to achieve its renewable energy goals. Wind farms were required to meet a 70% local content requirement.[5] The 2006 Renewable Energy Law required utilities to pay full price for electricity generated by renewable energy sources, and gave discounted rates to consumers. Indigenous innovation requirements introduced in 2006 reinforced the buy-domestic, buy-Chinese requirements throughout China's state-owned sector. In 2007, the Medium and Long-Term Development Plan for Renewable Energy in China set clean energy standards estimated to require non-hydro renewable energy installed power capacity of 3% by 2010 and 8% by 2010, causing investment in the renewables sector to surge. China's stimulus package emphasized renewable energy projects.[6] China continues to maintain very aggressive targets for energy conservation and emissions reduction in large part through rapid expansion in the installation of renewable energy capacity.[7] China's investments in renewable energy in 2009 exceeded those made by the United States for the first time.[8]

Table 1. Installed Clean Energy Capacity - Top 5 Countries
(Capacity in GW, data as of December 2011)

	China		U.S.		Germany		Spain		Italy		World
	GW	% World	GW	% World	GW	% World	GW	% World	GW	% World	
Wind	64	26.8%	47	19.7%	29	12.1%	22	9.2%	6.7	2.8%	239
Small-Hydro	62	33.7%	25.3	13.8%	1.9	1.0%	4.4	2.4%	5.8	3.2%	184
Solar	3	4.1%	4.6	6.3%	25	34.2%	5.3	7.3%	12.4	17.0%	73
Biomass	4	7.0%	13	22.8%	5.7	10.0%	0.9	1.6%	1.9	3.3%	57
Geothermal	0	0.0%	3.3	30.0%	0	0.0%	0	0.0%	0.87	7.9%	11
Marine	0	0.0%	0	0.0%	0	0.0%	0	0.0%	0	0.0%	0.6
Total	133	23.6%	93.2	16.5%	61.6	10.9%	32.6	5.8%	27.67	4.9%	564.6

Source: The Pew Charitable Trusts, *Who's Winning the Clean Energy Race? 2011 Edition* (2012).

The United States did lead the world in clean energy investment in 2011, followed by China, Germany and Italy. But this is a one-year snapshot. In 2011, U.S. investment amounted to $48.1 billion, largely in wind and solar power, coming in ahead of China's $45.5 billion for the first U.S. lead since 2008.[9]

---

[4] Clean energy is defined as wind, small-hydro, solar, biomass, geothermal and marine.

[5] The Notice of Requirements for the Administration of Wind Power Construction, National Development and Reform Commission, 2005.

[6] Renewable Energy Policy Update for China, Eric Martinot and Li Junfeng, Renewable Energy World, July 21, 2010.

[7] Ucilia Wang, China's Solar Master Plan Sets Production, Efficiency and Price Goals," Renewable Energy World.com (February 24, 2012); Damien Ma, "Energy Policy to Fuel Economic Objectives," China Daily (March 21, 2011); at http://www.gov.cn/zwgk/2011-09/07/content_1941731.htm.

[8] http://www.pewenvironment.org/uploadedFiles/PEG/Publications/Report/EXEC%20SUM_FINAL_LORES_WhoIsWinningTheCleanEnergyRace-REPORT-2012(1).pdf

[9] Bloomberg News Story on a Pew Charitable Trust finding. http://www.bloomberg.com/news/print/2012-04-12/u-s-clean-energy-policies-risk-losing-lead-over-china.html

TABLE 2: CLEAN ENERGY INVESTMENT BY
COUNTRY 2011 ($BILLION)

	2011 Investment	2010 Investment
U.S.	$48.0	$33.7
China	$45.5	$45.0
Germany	$30.6	$32.1
Italy	$28.0	$20.2
India	$10.2	$6.6
U.K.	$9.4	$7.0
Japan	$8.6	$7.0
Spain	$8.6	$6.9
Brazil	$8.0	$6.9

Source: The Pew Charitable Trusts, Who's Winning the Clean Energy Race? 2011 Edition (2012).

This is said by a number of observers to be short-lived:

> The [U.S.] jump to the top of the G-20 ranking followed developers' efforts to finish projects before incentives expire. With China taking on long-term renewable energy targets and an American tax-break for wind lapsing in 2012, the U.S. again risks losing its edge, said Phyllis Cuttino, Pew's clean energy director.
>
> "China is sending that important policy signal which the United States is failing to do to for investors. Even though China has fallen to number two, it seems as though investment there is going to continue at a very significant level for the foreseeable future. They are going to continue to be a dynamic clean-energy hub for the world."
>
> The U.S. doesn't have any comparable targets to China's goals of installing a total of 160 gigawatts of wind power and 50 gigawatts of solar power by 2020, she said. At the same time, a production tax credit benefiting wind producers expires at the end of the year. "In the absence of long-term policy, it's hard to see how the U.S. can grow significantly in the future. The boom-and-bust cycle of U.S. energy policy sends a very different signal to investors" from China.

The U.S. led in investment in the year 2011 when the Recovery Act had its greatest impact. Many of the Act's provisions have since expired. For example, section 1603 has retired; the 48c Manufacturing Tax Credit has not been renewed; and the DOE Loan Guarantee Program is not expected to make significant future loans. In addition, it is worth noting that U.S. deployment incentives like section 1603 did not require the use of domestic products, so deployment-oriented incentives had an effect in both the U.S. and Chinese markets

The Defense Department is the nation's largest consumer of energy. In April, the department announced a fairly low goal of using 3 gigawatts of renewable energy by 2025—enough to power three-quarters of a million homes. One gigawatt is to be developed for use by each service branch: the Air Force by 2016, the Navy by 2020, and the Army by 2025,[10] although the Army is likely to develop and use double that amount. As if to underline the uncertainties caused by U.S. policies supporting the development of renewable energy, three weeks ago the Senate Armed Services Committee adopted amendments to the National Defense Authorization Act seeking to limit the Department of Defense(DoD)'s use of domestically produced alternative energy. Potentially cutting in the other direction, on May 21, 2012, DOD issued a Defense Federal Acquisition Regulation Supplement to promote utilization of domestic photovoltaic devices under energy savings, utility service and housing contracts.[11]

Despite China's investments in renewables, DOE reports that renewables account for only 0.2% of China's electric power generation, and of that wind has the largest share.[12] At least until a few years ago, about 95% of China's PV production was

---

[10] http://www.examiner.com/article/renewables-for-the-military-part-1-congress-vs-defense-dept
[11] 77 Fed. Reg. 30368 (May 22, 2012).
[12] U.S. Energy Information Administration, Report on China, March 2012. Large-scale hydroelectric power represents 6% and nuclear power represents 1%. Coal is the largest source of energy consumption at 71% in 2008.http://www.eia.gov/countries/cab.cfm?fips=CH

exported, and China accounted for about 55% of the world production.[13] Today, the GTM Research estimate is that for 2012 about 25% of all Chinese PV module production will be consumed domestically, and 75% will be exported.

PROMOTING U.S. COMPETITIVENESS IN CLEAN TECH VIS-À-VIS CHINA

[T]he country fails to deploy into the marketplace the clean energy innovations it creates in the laboratory[14]

When Bell Labs was at its peak it was an idea factory that gave rise to whole industries in the United States, and led ultimately to the creation of the semiconductor industry.[15] Globalization, improved transportation, freer trade and the internet have created a world in which there is locational competition for the production of most industrial goods and services, and clean energy related equipment and materials is no exception. Given the U.S. failure to commercialize its inventions to the extent that we once did, the Committee on Comparative Innovation Policies of the National Academies has engaged in an intensive seven year effort to study best practices of other countries. In our forthcoming report, we will make a series of recommendations of factors determining the location of not only invention but production. These recommendations could easily be the subject of a series of separate hearings While the report does not focus on the renewable energy sector, it does point to the cross-sectoral policy reforms that the United States should consider in order to enhance the production within the United States of what is invented here. The recommendations are extensive—from the closer coordination of universities and the national laboratories with business, to manufacturing extension services and export promotion.

For renewable energy, more will be needed than simply greater efforts at export promotion or increasing manufacturing extension services. In most parts of the United States, clean energy for most applications is still more expensive than fossil fuel sources. Without subsidies and mandates, consumers will not choose clean energy, and private capital will not fund either research and development or deployment. A number of countries have promoted the installation of clean energy capacity with various types of subsidies (Germany, Spain, China, U.S., etc.) but budget constraints make a continuation of these policies difficult. This calls for even greater efforts to aggressively subsidize targeted R&D for clean energy to bring down the cost—making PV cells more efficient and wind turbines cheaper and more efficient, to take two examples. At the earliest stages of innovation, the U.S. remains very strong. We have some of the top research universities and national laboratories in the world. U.S. Government support for R&D has resulted in significant advances in these technologies, for example, the U.S. Department of Energy (DOE)-funded research over the past 35 years has yielded more than half of the world records in PV cell efficiency. Continued support for research and development can continue to lower the costs and improve performance for renewable energy technologies.

However, if this approach is taken alone, it will delay installation and use of clean energy capacity until it is economically feasible—or until a carbon tax is levied on fossil fuels to reflect their social cost. Neither are situations likely to exist in the near term. Therefore support throughout the industrial chain from R&D through to commercialization and deployment need to be considered. As strong as the U.S. is in innovation, there are costs to the economy if we fall behind in transitioning these technologies to domestically manufactured products. Even though we are a world leader in patents and research publications, U.S. manufacturing market share for PV cells and modules has fallen dramatically, from 43% market share in 1997 to less than 4% in 2011. R&D support by itself is not sufficient to develop a healthy domestic industry.

A comprehensive and cohesive policy should have at least three major elements: 1) an R&D strategy to lower costs and improve performance so that clean energy technologies can be truly competitive without the need for long term subsidies 2) a manufacturing strategy that incentivizes domestic production and job creation to ensure a healthy industrial ecosystem, and finally, 3) a deployment strategy that helps transition these new technologies into the marketplace and gradually phases out support as the technologies are able to compete without support.

---

[13] Cleantech citing industry sources uses the 95% figure. NREL data does not appear to contradict these statements. http://cleantechnica.com/2012/02/12/dumping-solar-study-sheds-light-on-solar-pv-trade-flows-us-china-manufacturing/

[14] http://www.pewenvironment.org/uploadedFiles/PEG/Publications/Report/EXEC%20SUM_FINAL_LORES_WhoIsWinningTheCleanEnergyRace-REPORT-2012(1).pdf

[15] The Idea Factory: Bell Labs And The Great Age Of American Innovation, Jon Gertner, Penguin Books Ltd, 2012.

Whether to make major public investments to accomplish these ends is an important subject for public policy debate. On the one hand, there are clearly fiscal constraints that exist now that were not present when the manned space flight program was announced. In addition, the current global industry is dominated by Chinese PV production, that even if dumped, is very low cost. On the other hand, U.S. innovation (and commercialization) from past national initiatives—whether from Bell Labs, NASA, DOE, NIH, or DOE and the national labs—have provided very substantial economic benefits, and support the commercial success of U.S. industry as well as ensuring growth in highly productive jobs.

Clearly, concentrated efforts by governments to support specific sectors have an effect on industrial development, whether here, China or in Europe. The staff of the Joint Committee on Taxation recently prepared a study on energy-related tax expenditures,[16] which I am sure that the Committee is familiar with. As noted above, the picture is one of an array of measures that are in most cases not of a reliably long duration. The electricity production credit provisions expire for wind at the end of this year. The Investment Tax Credit is considered to be at risk in tax reform given current fiscal pressures. The R&D tax credit is always extended on just a short term basis. The section 1603 Treasury Grant Program expired at the end of last year and is favored by the solar industry in preference to the advanced energy tax credit. The industry has also recommended that the Advanced Energy Manufacturing Tax Credit (MTC), which was over-subscribed, be renewed.[17]

The Department of Energy is making major efforts to support the development of solar energy, aiming to reduce the cost of solar energy systems by 75% before 2020. It seeks to enable widespread deployment of solar energy equipment in the U.S. without continuing subsidies. The SunShot Initiative is a business industry partnership with DOE funding support and with participation of universities and the national labs. The objectives are to return the U.S. to technological leadership, reduce energy costs generally, create employment, reduce greenhouse gas emissions and obtain a larger U.S. global market share. The Advanced Research Projects Agency—Energy (ARPA-E) within the Department of Energy (DOE) is also an important endeavor. The National Academy Report Rising Above the Gathering Storm stimulated and an authorization contained in passage of the America's Competes Act stimulated creation of ARPA-E. It was funded at a $400 million level through the American Recovery and Reinvestment Act (Recovery Act).[18] Its mission is to fund high risk energy research which holds some promise of dramatic results, and often to support public-private partnerships to do so. Future funding is not certain.

I cannot give you detailed prescriptions for tax and other measures to accomplish key renewable energy objectives. There are a number of government studies and industry papers laying out alternatives and recommendations that address these issues. But I have learned a few things in the course of studying and finding solutions to dealing with foreign industrial policies and the harm that they can cause to the U.S. industrial base. In particular, although the two sets of challenges are not alike in all respects, there are several informative parallels to be drawn between the successful effort to preserve America's future in semiconductors and the challenges posed by China's promotion of its renewable electrical generating equipment industry.

In the early 1980s, the Japanese market was largely closed to imports of semiconductors. Access to that market was essential for our industry to remain competitive as Japanese companies dominated the downstream consumer electronics industries that drove semiconductor demand and technological progress. Japanese government-sponsored R&D through MITI's and NTT's laboratories moved the industry down the learning curve in terms of process and product. The vertically integrated Japanese producers were selling semiconductors below their average cost of production in all markets. Full-blown industrial policies generally lead to the creation of excess capacity, and this was the case in memory chips (DRAMs). The Silicon Valley start-ups—Intel, AMD, National and others, were in danger of extinction.

There were a series of antidumping cases filed and large duties were to be applied. But trade remedies were not going to be a sufficient American response. For one thing, this would have been a one-market solution and the relevant market was global. Elimination of dumping in the United States alone would threaten the erosion of downstream industries. The antidumping trade solution would also be one-

[16] Present Law and Analysis of Energy-Related Tax Expenditures, Staff of the Joint Committee on Taxation, for the Subcommittee on Energy, Natural Resources and Infrastructure of the Senate Committee on Finance, March 23, 2012.

[17] See Manufacturing Solar Photovoltaic Products in the United States, the Semiconductor Equipment and Materials International (SEMI), 2012.

[18] ARPA-E's structure is codified in 42 U.S.C. 16538.

dimensional. The U.S. companies needed unencumbered access to foreign markets, they needed to improve their manufacturing skills, they needed to be able to engage in pre-competitive joint R&D to do so, they needed to continue to attract capital, they needed to improve the protection of their intellectual property, they needed to make sure that universities were training engineers with relevant skills and they needed tax policies that supported their voracious need for R&D spending. In short, a complete strategy was needed to ensure the competitiveness of the U.S. industry, not just trade measures.

There was a recognized U.S. national security interest in maintaining a leading edge American industry. The U.S. industry united around a series of domestic and trade policy responses and achieved buy-in from the Executive Branch and strong support from the Congress. All of the necessary measures were put into place. A U.S.-Japan agreement on semiconductors ultimately opened the Japanese market for foreign chips and precluded dumping by Japanese companies in any market. The antitrust laws were amended to provide a limited safe harbor for pre-competitive R&D, the Defense Department matched industry contributions at a rate of $100 million per year for five years to improve the manufacturing capability of the U.S. industry with the creation of Sematech (the semiconductor manufacturing technology initiative). A new form of intellectual property protection was created for maskworks. The R&D tax credit was extended.

This endeavor required consistency of effort on the part of both industry and government over a very extended period of time. The necessary programs, begun by the Reagan Administration, and vigorously supported by its free-market advocates including George Shulz and Clayton Yeutter, continued during Republican and Democratic administrations alike with strong bi-partisan Congressional support. It took six years to put all the measures into place and another decade to make them fully effective. It was the right mix of policies, but it took crafting a comprehensive approach and consistent dedication to implementation to achieve the desired result.

Today, semiconductors figure among the top categories of U.S. exports each year. Amazing new greenfield facilities costing upwards of $4 billion each can still be created here (for example, Global Foundries in Upstate New York). Industry employment is in the hundreds of thousands. And U.S. companies account for a majority share of global production, double their share in the early 1980s. Moreover, the years of turbulence have been replaced by years of international cooperation on public policies. The EU, Korea, Taiwan and China have joined together with Japan and the United States to eliminate tariffs on semiconductors, work on energy saving both in semiconductor production and through the use of semiconductors in other industries[19], and collaborate on improving a very good record with respect to environmental impact through reduction of chemical use. The industries support this effort through their World Semiconductor Council (WSC), bringing their joint recommendations to a Government and Authorities Meeting on Semiconductors (GAMS) annually.[20] Global competition is vigorous and semiconductors, doubling in functionality every eighteen months in accordance with Moore's law, have enabled the information revolution.

The relevance of the success of the policy responses in semiconductors to the challenges faced in the renewable energy sector require answers to a series of questions:

- First: Can it be demonstrated that there is a vital national interest at stake in maintaining a domestic manufacturing base for the tools to make solar energy cells and for their production, and for the production of wind turbines?
- Second: Is there a case to be made that joint pre-competitive R&D and/or other support would have the potential for yielding benefits important to the American economy?
- Third: If the first two answers are affirmative, what policy prescriptions should be implemented?

THE NATIONAL INTEREST

Although our current reliance on GPS, internet and wireless connectivity, I-Phones and hundreds of thousands of apps (applications) were at the time a quarter century away, the founders of the U.S. semiconductor industry had no doubt about whether their industry was vital to the nation's future. It took just over seven years

---

[19] See John A. "Skip" Laitner, Chris Knight, Vanessa McKinney, and Karen Ehrhardt-Martinez, Semiconductor Technology: The Potential to Revolutionize U.S. Energy Productivity, Research Report E094, May 1, 2009, American Council for an Energy Efficient Economy, athttp://aceee.org/research-report/e094

[20] See http://www.semiconductorcouncil.org/wsc/.

to get Washington to fully share this vision.[21] Factors leading to a consensus among policy makers included the fact that the country was locked in a Cold War with the Soviet Union and semiconductors had a central role to play in national defense. Moreover, the inherent unfairness of Japanese industrial policies, the closed Japanese home market together with U.S. industry's legal rights to at least stop the sales of Japanese semiconductors in the U.S. market at below cost of production, provided additional impetus to forming a U.S. consensus that a comprehensive response was necessary.

Can a national consensus be formed today on the following two points:

> 1) It is vitally important that clean energy account for a much greater share of U.S. energy supply—for reasons ranging from reducing the environmental impact of energy production and use to greater energy independence and therefore increased national security.

> 2) A complete U.S. domestic industrial production and supply chain is required to deliver clean energy efficiently—from R&D, to production of solar photovoltaic manufacturing equipment, materials such as polysilicon, modules, cells and turbines, through fabrication into panels and deployment into solar and wind farms—because the entire industry is vital to the American economy. Is it acceptable for Chinese industrial policies, including protection and subsidies, to result in that country being dominant in the technologies and products that yield clean energy? Can the country afford not to explore to find which clean energy technologies lie just beyond the horizon, to forego forever whatever new discoveries lie in the future?

We do not appear to be near a consensus yet that will drive a comprehensive solution to our clean energy requirements and the challenge posed by China's policies and objectives. The newly apparent plentiful availability of natural gas is diminishing one of the drivers of finding near term solutions. But that does not mean that a path forward cannot be found. Natural gas is actually complementary to renewable energy, as the sun does not always shine and the wind is not always constant. And there should at least be a national debate about whether government choices abroad should be allowed to shape the U.S. economy. That China chooses to have these industries should not mean that the United States should relinquish them. That said, there are a series of interests that also must be taken into account. The U.S. will not want to slow the deployment of low-cost renewable energy equipment. Deployment has important ramifications for climate change, jobs, sustainable development and economic growth. Upstream industries, supplying silicon and other materials and leading the world in making the tools that produce photovoltaics are also vitally important. The entire value chain must be taken into account.

SUPPORTIVE DOMESTIC POLICIES

The United States leads in the front end of innovation—invention—in the renewables sector. It has the most patents and the most research spending, but it has been losing out over the last decade in commercialization, in domestic manufacturing. This is a general problem for the United States, studied in depth by the National Academies in several of its projects, including the work on Comparative Innovation Policies. The creation of a substantial number of additional manufacturing jobs is a high priority and the renewable energy sector is a natural place to look to see what can be accomplished, because there is more than one broad national policy goal to be served in focusing on this sector.

The renewable energy industries require a stable and viable rate of return in order to maintain and attract capital. This can be achieved through a variety of measures—ameliorating excessive market distortions caused by low cost imports that are the product of foreign industrial policies; continuing supportive tax policies, use of direct subsidies, and the use of renewable energy standards. These measures are advocated in various publications of industry groups.

The solar photovoltaics industry shares some of the same technologies as the semiconductor industry. It uses silicon, chemical deposition, photo-lithography among other similarities. Whether Sematech—that is government co-funding of joint industry pre-competitive R&D—is a good model for this sector is well worth exploring.

---

[21] The U.S. Semiconductor Industry Association (SIA) was founded in 1977 by the co-inventor of the integrated circuit, Robert Noyce, CEO of Intel, Charlie Sporck, CEO of National Semiconductor, Jerry Sanders, CEO of Advanced Micro Devices (AMD), who were soon joined by John Welty of Motorola. The association was formed to better understand the foreign industrial policy challenge from Japan, and to collect and publish industry data.

Making renewable energies more cost competitive with fossil fuels should be approached not just from the side of creating demand and assuring an adequate rate of return, but also with the aim of making improvements in design and manufacturing technologies that will drive down costs. Those in the industry will have to decide whether they find a community of interest to engage in a common endeavor, and the government has to ascertain whether the national interest is served by spending more scare federal resources on an endeavor of this kind. It worked extraordinarily well for semiconductor manufacturing in the United States. And this joint endeavor led to other R&D efforts in this sector—to joint industry-government funding of university research through the Semiconductor Research Corporation (SRC), through Focus Center Research Program (FCRP) and Nanoelectronics Research Initiative (NRI). The industry also drove technological progress through creation of a technology roadmap—indentifying the technology challenges that would allow the creation of constantly increasing functionality.

Some questions that will have to be answered, that were answered in the affirmative for semiconductors and that resulted in the creation of a manufacturing technology research consortium are:

- Are either the competition from China a sufficient motivation for companies to engage in a common pre-competitive research endeavor or are there other external pressures that would cause them to do so?
- Is the ability to develop needed design technologies beyond the capability of any individual company?
- Is there a need to develop more effective manufacturing and process technology, leading to common testing and industry-wide standards?
- Can they achieve the necessary technology focus, determine the bounds of shared technology policy, and achieve effective means for technology transfer, while preserving vigorous competition?[22]

The renewables industries, and the PV-related industries alone—with a relatively large number of participants with a variety of interests, is far more fragmented than was the semiconductor industry in the 1980s: The PV industry is more global by far than the U.S. semiconductor industry was. There are well-established, important additional interests in the PV value chain. For example,. project developers may have less interest in technological development than PV producers have.

What is clear, and was enunciated by Gordon Moore, one of the founders of Intel, is that Sematech played a key role in reversing the X-curve that was the chief measure of semiconductor industry performance. This referred to a chart showing that U.S. producers once had a much greater share of the semiconductor market until 1985/86—having 57% to Japanese producers' 32%. But by 1988, Japanese share of worldwide production had climbed to about 52% and U.S. world share had dropped to around 27%. By 1991, there was another X cross over, and today, US share is about double that of the Japanese competition. Sematech delivered the necessary improvements in semiconductor-related technologies. When combined with other supportive public policies, Sematech proved to be highly effective.

Is there a need to support basic and applied R&D in renewables? We do not know where the technology will take us. We know that it is likely to improve efficiency of delivering renewables, but it can also result in dramatic breakthroughs and spin-offs, and this cannot be discounted. The applicability of the Sematech model deserves serious consideration.

CRAFTING AN APPROPRIATE U.S.-CHINA RELATIONSHIP ON CLEAN ENERGY

The trade relationship with China is complex. It is far from being free of problems but they do not dominate the relationship in the same way that the trade friction with Japan did in the 1970's to the early 1990s. China has been open to foreign investment since 1978 (although interference by the Chinese government is pronounced in some sectors) whereas Japan was completely closed during the period of trade problems. Japan was (and is) an ally; China is sometimes a partner and more often perhaps a rival. U.S businesses were largely united in their grievances against Japan. The U.S. private sector, including associations and even individual companies have divided interests with respect to China—seeing China as one of the world's largest growing markets, a major source of supply, a major location of foreign investment, often a difficult competitor and sometimes a difficult host country.

---

[22] See remarks of Clark McFadden and Gordon Moore in Securing the Future - Regional and National Programs to Support the Semiconductor Industry, Government Industry Partnerships Project, National Research Council of the National Academies, 2003.

During the earlier period I am using for comparison with China, Japan was only reluctantly and partially compliant with international trade rules. Chinese policies are still evolving. China had to change tens of thousands of laws and regulations to join the WTO, and to liberalize its economy very substantially in a very short time. And yet there is still an extensive list of barriers and market distortions with which foreign companies and their governments must contend. China accounts for the longest section of the U.S. Trade Representative's National Trade Estimates catalog of foreign trade and investment problems. Another difference in current trade relations with China as compared with earlier trade relations with Japan is that since the Uruguay Round was implemented in 1995, the United States has lost the freedom to retaliate whenever it made a unilateral judgment that its trade interests required it to do so. In addition, when the U.S. imposes trade measures, China has made it a practice to retaliate with its own trade actions which it seeks to justify under WTO rules, even if the measures it was responding to are fully justified under the WTO. Moreover, China has found the means to affect foreign trade in its pursuit of development of its industries in informal ways that are not necessarily as susceptible to being effectively remedied through WTO challenges.

In the case of imports into the United States of semiconductors from Japan, the dumping margins were prohibitive—trade in some products would have ceased. Through the use of U.S. section 301, unilateral trade retaliation was available to enforce an agreement. In contrast, with the WTO green energy equipment subsidies case brought by the U.S., although a positive WTO ruling was achieved, did not yield much in the way of practical results. The final dumping determinations will not be made in the solar polysilicon case until the Fall, but if the duties and rates are along the lines of the preliminary findings (30-34% for dumping margins for 90% of the trade, a few percent for subsidy rates), the trade remedy may not be enough to change the serious situation in which the solar industry finds itself—since the decline in solar PV prices over the last eighteen months has been about double those percentages.

A complicating factor of antidumping relief is that it affects only shipments from one country. If the Chinese producers assemble panels in third countries, source cells from Taiwan, or set up factories in third countries, the trade remedy will likely not cover some or all of those shipments.

There is authority in the Commerce Department to work out a "suspension agreement" to waive the duties in return for potentially a quantitative restriction and a price floor covering China's shipments of the subject merchandise.[23][24] This is perhaps possible to achieve if the Chinese government (which has effective control in this sector) believes that the final margins will be prohibitively high, and that it serves China's policy interests to enter into an arrangement of this kind (which it has done in some other cases prior to its entry into the WTO). While the domestic industry does not have a veto over these arrangements, it is consulted, and it is politically difficult for the U.S. government to compromise away what is taken in our legal system to be a right to trade relief—unless the alternative is equally or more attractive to the petitioning domestic industry.

Had the U.S. antidumping case been coordinated with a trade case brought by the European Commission, something that has not to my knowledge ever happened, there would perhaps be more interest on the part of China in a settlement. Given the short time until the final determination at Commerce, the likelihood of a negotiated settlement by this Fall is probably close to nonexistent. It is not clear that sufficient inducements can be found to bring about an agreement to stabilize this trade. A settlement later is, however, possible—especially with the consent of the U.S. petitioner industry.

---

[23] 19 USC 1673c provides in relevant part:
(l) Special rule for nonmarket economy countries
(1) In general
The administering authority may suspend an investigation under this part upon acceptance of an agreement with a nonmarket economy country to restrict the volume of imports into the United States of the merchandise under investigation only if the administering authority determines that—
(A)such agreement satisfies the requirements of subsection (d) of this section, and
(B)will prevent the suppression or undercutting of price levels of domestic products by imports of the merchandise under investigation.
d) Additional rules and conditions The administering authority may not accept an agreement under subsection (b) or (c) of this section unless—
(1)it is satisfied that suspension of the investigation is in the public interest, and
(2)effective monitoring of the agreement by the United States is practicable.
[24] Examples of antidumping suspension agreements entered into with Chinese exporters include: Honey From the P.R.C., 60 Fed. Reg. 42,521 (ITA Aug. 16, 1995); Cut-to-length Plate from the PRC, 62 Fed. Reg. 61774 (1997).

What factors would militate toward a possible settlement? Are there common interests that can grow out of the following common objectives?

- Both China and the United States wish to deploy much more in the way of renewables, enhancing the role of renewables in the mix of their energy consumption.
- Both China and the United States seek to see the price of PV modules decline through increased efficiencies in both solar and wind to foster this objective.
- Both countries wish to maintain and nurture the industries that produce the supply chain for renewables.
- Both countries wish to foster the development of relevant technologies at home.

Despite having a number of interests in common, a trade skirmish is brewing. In the fall the U.S. will likely impose antidumping duties on Chinese exports. This is not a minor amount of trade, an estimated 2 gigawatts worth of solar modules were shipped into North America in 2012 from Chinese manufacturers, representing as much as 60 percent of the market, and about $3 billion in trade.[25] Three weeks ago today the Chinese Ministry of Commerce pronounced six renewable energy support measures granted by the states of Washington, Massachusetts, Ohio, New Jersey and California were grants as inconsistent with the WTO rules. Of course, U.S. shipments of renewable energy generating equipment such as wind turbines or solar modules to China is small compared with Chinese shipments of solar cells and modules to the United States—but the U.S. has strong export interests in the equipment to make solar cells, in exports of polysilicon and exports of high-value parts for wind turbines.

What are China's principal interests? The most obvious immediate interest would be Chinese producers would wish to avoid making very large cash deposits in the U.S. Treasury for a long time to come on their exports . There is also the degree of uncertainty as to what the ultimate duty liability will be, which if the Chinese did not adjust their prices or cease shipping (the latter being extremely unlikely) would be very large. Trade does not thrive with uncertainty. Moreover, with a U.S. antidumping duty order in place on PV, the pressure on the European market will increase, perhaps triggering antidumping action there. (India may follow suit as well). There might be broader Chinese interests about cooperation on R&D in the area of renewables. It also may be that price stability with respect to exports would be in line with and reinforce any Chinese government plans to rationalize domestic overcapacity in wind and solar and increase its deployment of renewable energy sources both in terms of grid-connected and residential uses.

What are America's principal interests? The U.S. government is committed in principle to allowing industries to petition for trade relief and to receive it where warranted under the law. This is consistent with WTO rules where domestic industries are harmed by dumped or subsidized trade. That said, trade measures are only a very partial solution to strengthening the domestic U.S. renewables industries. To foster the deployment of renewable energy equipment and the industry producing the tool, equipment and materials for this equipment, there has to be a reasonable rate of return to continue to attract necessary capital. This objective can be served by a predictable and consistent level of support in terms of tax policy, DOE investments, feed in tariffs and clean energy standards. To reduce the need for financial supports and mandates through clean energy standards, the costs of producing renewable energy need to decline. Harnessing the research capabilities of universities and the private sector in a common effort to achieve this objective needs to be seriously considered. A potentially useful model has been provided by the interaction between the private sector and the U.S. government with respect to semiconductors.

Ultimately trade measures and domestic policies should be integrated and a strategic approach crafted to the U.S.-China clean energy set of problems. If there is an attempt at a grand bargain, access to the Chinese market for wind turbines produced outside China should be part of any overall settlement.

Would China avoid talks because it would not want the precedent established of its agreeing to settle antidumping cases with quantitative restrictions and minimum price provisions? Would it do so from fear that agreeing to a suspension agreement might lead to other calls for export restraints by China? It is hard to predict. I know of no instance where China has settled an antidumping order with the U.S. with export restraints since China joined the WTO. However, China, it should be assumed, can be pragmatic if it sees the balance of its interests served by a settlement, particularly if it were part of a very broad package. One consistent Chinese demand is that the U.S. liberalize its export controls. While the United States will

[25] http://www.isuppli.com/photovoltaics/pages/headlines.aspx.

not compromise its national security to reach any agreement with China, extensive technology-sharing actually takes place now, although informally, through foreign investment. Perhaps there is something in the technology arena—R&D with respect to clean coal or carbon sequestration—that would be of mutual interest and that could be added to an agreement providing for the complete elimination of dumping. This might occur through a broader program or with more resources than currently exist for the U.S.-China Clean Energy Research Center (CERC).

Medium term, and not likely in the next few months, a trilateral (U.S.-China-EU) renewables accord might create added interest for China. My assumption is that none of the three—the U.S., China or the EU—is prepared to see the growth of its domestic renewables industries curtailed given its energy policy objectives? The World Semiconductor Council and the Governments and Authorities Meeting on Semiconductors may be models that can be employed to promote cooperation at the industry and government levels on mutually beneficial public policies. In that all three regions are supporting their renewables sector, it may be that a trade agreement makes some sense, incorporating and superseding antidumping relief.

The bottom line: It is not yet clear that sufficient inducements can be found to bring about an agreement providing for equitable trade that fosters long-term growth in these industries. This does not mean that there should not be further consideration given to the possibilities, and efforts made to find common ground Whatever the possibilities are of reaching an accommodation with China on PV, there is an overriding U.S. national interest in assuring that new leading edge technologies are developed and manufactured in this country, or we will lose the ability to do so. As the United States is the world's most innovative country, that would be a loss not just for the United States but for a world in which renewable energy sources must account for an increasing proportion of the supply of growing energy needs.

The CHAIRMAN. Thank you very much.

Mr. Prestowitz, thank you for coming. We appreciate it.

STATEMENT OF CLYDE PRESTOWITZ, PRESIDENT, ECONOMIC STRATEGY INSTITUTE

Mr. PRESTOWITZ. Thank you, Mr. Chairman. It's my pleasure to be here. I thank you, Senators Murkowski, Wyden, and Franken, as well.

You've asked what is the current landscape of China's investment and it's been delineated a bit by the previous two speakers. I'd like to describe it in the following way. I think China is committed to developing clean and renewable energy technology in the same way that the United States is committed to achieving air superiority aircraft as part of its pivot to Asia. That is to say it's a high national priority. That is to say that the United States Air Force is not thinking of turning to European or Asian suppliers to supply its No. 1 strike aircraft.

Developing this technology and leadership in this industry in China is a matter of the highest national security, and China is not thinking of it in terms of Adam Smith, David Ricardo free trade, laissez faire, comparative advantage.

I say that because that has to inform then our own response to China, and I want to emphasize, not just China. I remember in February 2009 I was invited to a White House meeting to discuss the future of green technology in the Obama Administration, and there was a debate between those who—in the administration, who wanted to become proactive with various kinds of incentives to promote green energy and other, more traditionally market-oriented officials who argued that we don't want to pick winners and losers, that we should rely on market incentives solely.

The point I made in that discussion was: Are you kidding me? I look around the world and I see Germany has a huge program subsidizing solar technology, and Denmark has a big program subsidizing wind power technology, and Japan is doing batteries and solar and wind power, and Korea is doing batteries, and China is doing batteries and wind power and solar, and I said: That's the market.

So when you say leave it to the market, you're saying leave it to the tender mercies of German, Japanese, Korean, Chinese, Norwegian industrial policy.

So when we ask ourselves what is an appropriate American reaction or response now, that same situation pertains. We're not living in a world of open market free trade here. This is not Adam Smith. We're living in an environment in which industrial policy is defining the outlines of the market and the incentives.

So, that being the case, it seems to me that the first major question that we the United States have to answer is: How important do we think it is for the United States to have a capability in these technologies. When I say capability, I mean a technological capability, that is an understanding of the technology and the ability to do research in the technology and somehow to remain at the leading edge of the research.

But also, because it's often difficult to remain at that leading edge without some competitive productive capability, then the question also arises to what extent is it necessary for us to have a commercially productive, competitive, productive capability. That question has to be asked not for the short term, but for the long term, because the nature of these kinds of industries is that they're characterized by economies of scale, by doing by learning, by past dependence.

So you don't get to there unless you've kind of gone through the preliminary steps. You don't make huge leaps ahead without having had the preliminary experience.

So if we think that these technologies are really going to be important down the road, even if, for example, the low price of shale gas undercuts them today, but maybe that's a temporary phenomenon—if they're going to be important down the road, then it's necessary to adequately identify the incentives and disincentives in the market that are being created by the industrial policies of our various competitors and trading partners and by our own and adjust them in such ways as to assure that there's a continuing competitive U.S. capability.

Now, as my colleague Alan Wolff pointed out, this is not a new question. This is not a new phenomenon. We've been here before. We saw this in the seventies and eighties with Japan and more recently in the nineties and aughties with others, Japan, Korea, Taiwan, Singapore. All of them have adopted similar kinds of proactive industrial development policies to achieve their miracles and to achieve dominance in industries that used to be dominated by the U.S., and, let me under strike, in industries that are capital-intensive, labor-intensive—I mean, not labor-intensive, capital-intensive, technology-intensive, not labor-intensive.

So those are the industries in which we keep telling ourselves, our top economists keep telling us, that we are competitive in capital-intensive and technology-intensive industries. But what we keep seeing is loss of competitiveness in those industries in the face of the policies of some of these I've mentioned.

However, as Alan rightly points out, we in the case of Japan in the semiconductor industry, there was a recognition in the U.S. of a need to respond and we did respond. It wasn't a perfect response, but, as Alan pointed out, the United States retains a very powerful leading edge capability in the semiconductor industry.

How did we respond? With a broad, comprehensive policy. We self-initiated. Let me say the word again: self-initiated. That is, the White House didn't wait for industry to bring a complaint. The White House filed a complaint against Japanese dumping of semiconductors. So an antidumping case, but it wasn't just an anti-dumping case.

We created Sematech as an industry-government consortium to promote cooperation and collaboration among device makers, equipment makers, in order to foster the advance of that nexus and the advance of leadership in the equipment industry.

We had the Plaza Agreement, which resulted in a revaluation of the vastly undervalued Japanese yen. So a whole range, panoply of measures, comprehensively linked together to deal with the question of how do we stay competitive in this industry. We had an agreement with Japan, the so-called semiconductor agreement, under which the Japanese, No. 1, agreed to halt their dumping, but, No. 2, also committed to seeing to it that foreign producers got a fair share of the Japanese market, defined as about 20 percent, which in fact we did get.

So that I think is indicative of the kind of policy approach, the kind of attitudinal response, that's called for in this situation with China, and, again I say, not just China, but in the world of clean energy, particularly in Asia.

Thank you.

[The prepared statement of Mr. Prestowitz follows:]

PREPARED STATEMENT OF CLYDE PRESTOWITZ, PRESIDENT, ECONOMIC STRATEGY INSTITUTE

Good morning Chairman Bingaman, Senator Murkowski, members of the Committee. Thank you for the opportunity to testify before the Committee this morning on this very timely topic.

This morning I would like to take a slightly different tack than some of the other witnesses. Rather than look at some of the current opportunities and issues that the United States and China face in green technology space, I want to provide some historical perspective that I think will be useful. There is a cliché that history tends to repeat itself. I think this is one of those cases.

I was recently reminded of a conversation I participated in that took place in Vice President Biden's office in the early days of the Obama administration about how to put together the President's upcoming stimulus proposal. Part of the overall discussion dealt with the role of clean technologies and the possibility of using green jobs as one of the lynch pins of the program.

The room split into two camps. On one side, you had environmental activists who argued for a strong government role in helping these relatively nascent industries grow and flourish. On the other side, you had conventional economists making the opposite point that we should allow the markets determine which industries would succeed. These economists pulled out the old line about the government not picking winners and losers.

I felt a sense of déjà vu. I remembered having this exact same conversation more than 25 years ago when I worked in the Reagan administration.

After all, we have faced this question before in other industries, especially in the semiconductor industry in the 1980s with regard to Japan. In those days, Japan targeted key industries for development as part of its industrial policy. It protected them at home, provided special investment incentives and preferred financing, and promoted their exports also with special tax incentives and by maintaining an undervalued currency. The result was massive overinvestment and excess capacity in Japan that was dumped into the U.S. market.

The United States faced the question of whether this dumping was a gift to consumers or a force for destruction of an industrial capability of vital long term importance. We also faced the question of whether the gift would always be given or whether once Japan reached dominance, prices in the United States would rise to Japanese levels. It is important that we remember the lessons learned from our issues with Japan in the 1980s when dealing with China.

In my opinion, this debate shows a continued fundamental misunderstanding of the way the world works. Rather rehashing the same old debate for the ten thousandth time, we need to realize that many of our trading partners are already intervening in the market. Whether it is China, Japan, Korea or Germany, all of these countries have long ago put in place policies—dare I say industrial policies—to promote these industries. They see clean tech industries—solar, wind, batteries and others—as the industries of the future and have put policies in place to support them.

Although China is not the only country that put policies into place to support their clean tech industries, it is one of the most aggressive.

One powerful element of China's industrial policy strategy is the 863 Program, a project launched in March 1986 (863 is the year and date of the project's birth) by China's then paramount leader Deng Xiaoping to drive its technological catch-up effort. In 2001 this program began to focus intensely on energy, especially new or green energy, setting targets for installing wind turbines, solar panels, hydroelectric dams, and other renewable resources. In 2006 the 863 Program drove China to double its wind power capacity, and then it doubled again the following year and again the year after that. In 2003 China had virtually no solar power industry. By 2008, it was making more solar cells than any other country and taking customers away from American and other foreign companies that had originally invented the technology.

In October 2009, President Hu commented that China must "seize preemptive opportunities in the new round of the global energy revolution." In response, U.S. Assistant Secretary of Energy David Sandalow acknowledged that "unless the U.S. makes investments, we are not competitive in the clean-tech sector in the years and decades to come." Not only did 863 provide funding but it also required that wind farms, for example, use locally manufactured equipment. The fact that this requirement went into effect in 2003 and was dropped in 2009 is instructive. In 2003, China was a high-cost producer. By 2009, it had achieved such economies of scale and advanced in technology sufficiently that it was the low-cost producer. Dropping the "buy Chinese" rule then had no effect. By now everyone was buying Chinese because they were the cheapest and of good quality.

Interestingly, the 863 Program was fashioned after similar programs at the U.S. National Institutes of Health and the Pentagon's Defense Advanced Research Projects Agency. Since the program got rolling in 1987, its budget has grown by more than fifty times.

Thanks to the research from Bloomberg New Energy Finance, we also know about the large amounts of subsidies the central and provincial governments have provided Chinese companies. A new World Bank report, co-authored with the Development Research Center of the State Council (DRC), reports that the Chinese government considers its solar and wind power industry—along with its nascent solar polysilicon industry—to be state controlled. We also know that the Chinese have instituted policies, recently updated in the most recent Five Year Plan released earlier this year, to support these industries and provide some level of coordination.

There are specific plans for each of the individual clean tech sectors, but for illustrative purposes, I would like to focus on the plan for China's solar industry.

The recently published solar plan, which covers the period through 2015, reflects the Chinese government's resolve to ensure the industry's continued rapid development by directly managing its planning, policy and growth. According to one of the publicly available translations of the latest plan, the Chinese government once again designated its solar sector as one of seven "strategic emerging industries." As a result, the Plan calls for significant government financial assistance, preferential treatment and significant oversight. This includes new financial and price subsidies; more support in industry, financial and tax policy; and further aid with development and production of equipment used to produce polysilicon, silicon ingots, wafers, cells and panels within the crystalline-silicon solar industry. Moreover, the portfolio includes plans to support industrialization of China's as-yet-undeveloped thin-film industry, specifically harnessing silicon and copper indium gallium diselenide solar technologies.

The new Five-Year Plan also provides even greater support for exports than previous government plans. The 2011-2015 plan calls for identifying and promoting "national champions." It aims for consolidation of "the industry's position in the international market," partly so that "Chinese PV enterprises' international influence will be greatly enhanced" and be better able "to cope with international competition and market risks."

The programs the Chinese lay out in their new Five-Year Plan are not necessarily bad and, per the request of the Committee, I will not comment as to whether they are WTO-legal or not.

The more important point is that the Chinese government had a plan that helped its solar industry to grow from a non-factor in the industry to the world's largest producer on solar in less than a decade. It is now moving forward with the next generation of a program that consolidates these gains.

So, what do we need to do? Again, I believe history has an answer.

To the extent that the United States and China can work together to develop new technologies through non-commercial research, we should applaud and support these programs. Programs such as the U.S.-China Clean Energy Research Center (CERC), funded by the U.S. Department of Energy, could have a significant long-term impact. As we have learned through programs such as DARPA, Sematech and the new ARPA-E, there is a role for the government to play in this process and these programs can be extremely successful.

However, there is much more that we need to look at doing if we, as a nation, decide we want to be players in the clean tech industries in the future.

I believe that we need our own program to support industries we deem important—and I believe clean tech is important. This is not, as the conventional economists I mentioned at the start of my testimony claim, picking winners and losers. We are already doing that—we just don't want to say we do it using those loaded terms. Indeed, we should not worry about these criticisms. We need to accept them, move on and enact policies that will help American manufacturers and promote global innovation.

Although the United States eschews a formal economic strategy and any kind of stated industrial policy, we have such policies. We cannot avoid having a de facto economic strategy and de facto industrial policies of all kinds.

For example, the FCC must choose how to regulate telecommunications. The choice of focusing on competition (a process) rather than on deployment (a result) is a form of industrial policy—or perhaps of anti-industrial policy.

I would argue that for the government to stand to the side and do nothing is a de facto industrial policy of the worst kind. We are in effect saying we don't care where the next generation of clean technologies are designed and built. We are willing to step aside and let another country dominate a sector. We are also saying we are sticking with the status quo and continuing our reliance on imported oil and dirty coal.

I would argue that the ongoing existence of DARPA, ARPA-E, and the National Institutes of Health and many other agencies and programs is an example of current U.S. industrial policies. The U.S. government is very large, spends an enormous amount of money, and sets standards and regulations that have an enormous impact on the business environment, on the shape of various industries, and on the conditions of consumer life.

As a result, I believe there is a significant role that the U.S. government can play that will support the development of an American—and global—clean tech industry.

The United States government did this back in the 1980s. In order to help American manufacturers deal with Japan's industrial policy that specifically targeted the semiconductor industry, the federal government enacted a wide variety of initiatives. I would like to list four, along with their current policy equivalents.

- In 1985, the United States, in conjunction with the France, Japan, United Kingdom and West Germany, negotiated the Plaza Agreement. By reducing the value of the American dollar, a Republican administration was able to help make American exports more price competitive. This, in turn, allowed American companies to continue to invest and improve their products so that could become more competitive in the global marketplace. Unfortunately, even this significant agreement was not enough.

  We are seeing the same thing today with China. Both the Bush and Obama administrations have gone out of their way to avoid labeling China a currency manipulator. While the Chinese government has made a few moves to increase the value of their currency, its recent decision to devalue its currency in order to prop up exports is a sign that jawboning and looking the other way will not work. We need an aggressive currency policy, enacted in conjunction with our allies, in order to ensure change.

- We used the purchasing power of the federal government to build a market for semiconductors and, when necessary, codified this preference through "Buy American" laws.

  Although conventional economists eschew such rules, they are WTO-legal as they long we include products made by countries that have signed the WTO Government Procurement Protocol. This still gives many of our global competitors in solar access to the American government marketplace. However, it does send a signal that we believe it is important where we purchase products, especially for the military.

- The federal government also took a strong look at using our trade laws to remove market distorting measures enacted by the Japan government and Japanese manufacturers that both helped American companies in our market and worked to open up the Japanese market to competition. This included self-initiating an anti-dumping case against Japanese semiconductor manufacturers and negotiating the 1986 Semiconductor Agreement. We also learned to stay vigilant, as we learned that the Japanese government replaced official trade barriers, such as tariffs, with non-tariff barriers, such as production subsidies and government-industry collusion.

  In cases where we believe our competitors are not playing by the rules, we should not hesitate to push to use our trade laws. Last year, President Obama, acting on a complaint by the United Steelworkers, spoke out against Chinese practices in the wind power sector his administration thought were WTO illegal. By taking the Chinese to the World Trade Organization, the administration was able to get the Chinese to agree to stop subsidizing wind power firms that used Chinese-made parts at the expense of imports. The administration's decision, in conjunction with the European Union and Japan, to force China to lift export limits on rare earth minerals, is another example. As the Committee knows, rare earths are important parts of green technologies such as wind turbines, hybrid car batteries, and energy-efficient lighting. Finally, should the government take action against China, or any one or our other trading partners, we must ensure U.S. Customs and Border Protection has the resources it needs to prevent circumvention.

- We developed government initiatives to help support our domestic manufacturers through funding basic, non-commercial research and development. Sematech is just one example of a successful program. As the Chairman knows, we also gave wider latitude to our national laboratories to work with industry as opposed to only focusing on government problems. A Democratic Congress passed, and President George H.W. Bush, signed the High Performance Computing and Communication Act of 1991. This one piece of legislation helped put in place many of the necessary building blocks of the Internet we know today, including high-speed fiber optic networks and the Mosaic browser.

  In addition to funding the China Clean Energy Research Center, I also believe that we should take a serious look at increasing support for the U.S. Photovoltaic Manufacturing Consortium, a U.S. research consortium built along the lines of, and with the support of, SEMATECH. I was an early proponent of SEMATECH and continue to believe that these types of programs that solve common manufacturing problems by leveraging resources and sharing risks are helpful in ensuring that we leverage the power of our corporate and university R&D to help American industry.

The challenge we face is that if we want the United States to remain competitive globally in clean technologies, we need to do something that is rare in Washington these days. We need to be bold.

There are opportunities to work with China and the United States government should explore them, just as we would with any other country. But we should remember that the Chinese government has a policy to not just be a leader in a number of technologies, but the leader. The United States must determine how we are going to respond and decide how much we want to be a leader. With strong action, we have the opportunity to develop a globally competitive industry in a sector that has great promise both economically and environmentally. Without it, we face a future where the United States is sitting on the sidelines.

Thank you again for this opportunity and I look forward to your questions.

The CHAIRMAN. Thank you very much.

Mr. Holladay, you're the person who's expert on Sematech, so you can correct the previous witnesses and give us your view.

STATEMENT OF DAN W. HOLLADAY, DIRECTOR, ADVANCED TECHNOLOGIES AND PV PROGRAMS, SEMATECH

Mr. HOLLADAY. Thank you very much, and thank you for inviting me here today to speak on these important topics. We at Sematech deeply appreciate your leadership, Mr. Chairman, Senator Murkowski, Senator Franken, Senator Wyden, on these matters of industrial competitiveness that are so important to our continued growth and prosperity.

We are facing challenges today that are comparable to the late 1980s, which my colleagues have spoke on here, when Sematech was established. At a time when both industry and government budgets were tight, foreign producers have captured key high tech product markets and are rapidly developing the know-how and the capacity to capture next generation technologies.

The U.S. has always led in R and D and there has been a broad consensus that science and technology are integral to economic growth. In recent decades, however, the relationship between R and D and manufacturing has been less well understood. While we as a nation still lead the world in discovery, we do face a real danger of becoming a producer of intellectual property that is ultimately commercialized elsewhere. Such an outcome denies the American economy the tremendous economic benefit that comes with manufacturing, transforming IP into products, resulting in both revenue and jobs.

As we face stiff competition and severe budget pressures, the Sematech story is particularly instructive. In 1987, Congress authorized the bold Sematech experiment and public-private partnership and subsequently appropriated $100 million per year, matched dollar for dollar by industry, to fund an industry-led consortium of leading chipmakers to help restore U.S. leadership in semiconductors.

By the mid-1990s, Sematech had accomplished its mission and withdrawn from Federal funding. The experiment had succeeded and, through collaborative programs to improve manufacturing tools and processes, Sematech had indeed played a key role in pulling the industry together and reestablishing U.S. competitiveness in the global market. Even now, 25 years later, the Sematech experience as an industrial consortium is one of successfully facilitating collaboration in pre-competitive R and D. Sematech memberships, cooperatively funded, conduct projects to fill key gaps in R and D and manufacturing, developing key tools, materials, processes, and providing testbeds to facilitate demonstration and evaluation of innovations in production.

This experience of groundbreaking industry consortium support by public and private funding is directly applicable to many critical industries today, including photovoltaics, energy storage, smart grid, cyber security systems, biomedical devices, MIMS and NIMS devices, biofuels, nanomaterials, and others.

Such a consortium has these important attributes: It's based on sharing costs and risk and collective intelligence. Bob Noyce said: "Knowledge is power, but knowledge shared is power multiplied."

It is industry-led, member-driven, assuring that its direction and decisions are attuned to the industry's priorities and to the market. It allows for both collaborative programs and proprietary work with IP protection.

Its broad representation of the industry supply chain creates a critical mass and ability to drive consensus, develop road maps, and provide industry direction from a collective voice.

It is built on public-private partnerships that leverage both government and industry funding. Initial government funding acts as a catalyst, while industrial funding increases over time and moves the consortium toward financial self-sufficiency.

It bridges research, development, and manufacturing, pulling the research into the mainstream, providing manufacturing development facilities similar to what EERE is working on with their advanced manufacturing office. It provides facilities for testing and prototyping at scale, which is very critical, and accelerating the creation of advanced production lines in the U.S. and commercialization of new materials, equipment, and products.

It's a national initiative, but with selective international collaboration, especially in areas such as environmental safety and health, standards, reliability. We have proven methodologies to collaborate internationally and still protect U.S. manufacturing-based IP.

Sematech has evolved over its 25-year history to keep pace and help lead this dynamic semiconductor industry. We have expanded our program's scope and our engagement with the supply chain and diversified our funding sources as we develop next generation equipment and technology platforms, such as extreme UV lithography programs, novel transistor materials, 3D devices, and now the transition to 450-millimeter wafers.

At the same time, we're starting to apply Sematech's experience to new technology areas with manufacturing challenges. Last year Sematech was selected by the Department of Energy to establish the U.S. Photovoltaic Manufacturing Consortium, PVMC, to establish and accelerate the development of and commercialization and manufacturing of next generation solar photovoltaic systems. Keeping with Sematech's model and proven best practices, PVMC will provide collaborative consortium R and D programs, as well as manufacturing development facilities to test and demonstrate new technologies and manufacturing processes at production scale, which once again is very critical.

In conclusion, in our view a Sematech-like model for collaboration with a catalyst of public-private partnerships must be part of the U.S. play book to leverage unique U.S. advantages in innovations and strengthen the bridge between R and D and manufacturing. In addition, to leverage our country's strong universities, national labs, and venture capital system, we as a nation must nurture disruptive technology development and robust manufacturing if we are to build the infrastructure for sustainable growth and leadership in the global economy.

Thank you.

[The prepared statement of Mr. Holladay follows:]

28

PREPARED STATEMENT OF DAN W. HOLLADAY, DIRECTOR, ADVANCED TECHNOLOGIES
AND PV PROGRAMS, SEMATECH

Thank you for inviting me here today to speak on this important topic. On behalf of all of us at SEMATECH, I would also like to offer our heartfelt gratitude to you, Mr. Chairman, for your strong support over the years. We well remember your efforts in the early years, not only to support our funding, but also to advocate for the principles of industry autonomy and management, which have been so critical to our ultimate success. Your vision was prescient then, and now, twenty-five years later, you are still asking the right questions. Senator Murkowski, we so deeply appreciate your commitment to our nation's energy security and your leadership in supporting efforts to improve our industrial competitiveness.

Today we find ourselves once again facing stiff global competition as well as severe budget pressure. I understand the Committee's charge to be: what can we do affirmatively to improve our industrial competitiveness. We believe the SEMATECH experience is a big part of the answer.

Even in the midst of a historic global economic slowdown, the US remains the font of innovation, leading the world in patents, and indeed, garnering as many patents as the rest of the world combined. While we lead the world in discovery, we do face a real danger of becoming merely a producer of intellectual property that is ultimately commercialized elsewhere. Such an outcome denies the American economy the tremendous economic benefit that comes with transforming IP into products—both revenues and jobs—and ultimately denies the American taxpayer a return on the investments in the underlying research. Several trends, including outsourcing and growing competition from low cost producers overseas have eroded the U.S. industrial base and, along with it, the engineering and manufacturing capabilities needed to produce next generation products. Erosion in know-how, skilled personnel, and the supplier base has jeopardized or contributed to the loss of U.S. leadership in several key hightech products including solar cells. Foreign producers now dominate these component and product markets, and are rapidly developing the know-how and capacity to capture next generation technologies.

The United States cannot cede leadership in future game-changing technologies such as nanotechnology-based products, smart materials, biopharmaceuticals, energy storage, and digital devices for ubiquitous computing. Both our economic and our national security depend on our industrial competitiveness. But, increasingly, development of leading edge products is intertwined tightly with manufacturing know-how and development of production processes. Simply put, the erosion of U.S. manufacturing capacity must be reversed to preserve America's ability to innovate.

THE SEMATECH MODEL

The competitive challenges we are facing today—while formidable—are not unprecedented. We have faced similar challenges before and we have met them. The conditions that gave rise to SEMATECH—most notably our trade deficit with Japan—were similarly daunting. Twenty-five years later, the SEMATECH story shows us that industrial consortia are both necessary and effective. But at that time, much of what we now know was in question. Whether the government should fund SEMATECH to help bolster the U.S. semiconductor industry, and how involved the government should be in SEMATECH's operations were seriously debated issues. The strength of the foreign competition and DOD's interest in having a domestic supply of both semiconductor devices and equipment, however, drove the government to undertake this public-private partnership that has since become the standard for many others.

In 1987, Congress authorized the bold SEMATECH (SEmiconductor MAnufacturing TECHnology) experiment, and subsequently appropriated $100M per year, matched dollar for dollar by industry, to fund an industry-led consortium of leading chipmakers to help restore U.S. leadership in semiconductors. By the mid-1990's, SEMATECH had accomplished its mission and withdrawn from federal funding; the bold experiment had succeeded, and through collaborative programs to improve manufacturing tools and processes, SEMATECH had indeed played a key role in pulling the industry together and re-establishing U.S. competitiveness in the global market.

Today, twenty-five years after its founding, SEMATECH is a global consortium of semiconductor device, equipment, and materials manufacturers, continuing to explore ways to advance current semiconductor manufacturing technologies and build the infrastructure for emerging next-generation technologies, to transform novel ideas into manufacturable and marketable solutions. SEMATECH's long-time mission has been to focus on pre-competitive or noncompetitive R&D—cooperatively developing standards, building infrastructure, assuring that key components (tools, materials, processes) are in place when needed by industry—always with an eye toward improving manufacturability and accelerating commercialization. With strong support of the State of New York, where we are headquartered, we work closely with a collaborative network of over 150 global partners—including our strategic partners, the College of Nanoscale Science and Engineering of the University (CNSE) at Albany, as well as semiconductor companies, equipment and materials manufacturers, national laboratories, universities, research institutes and other organizations throughout the industry ecosystem—to leverage resources and develop innovative research, development, and manufacturing solutions. Through SEMATECH, members cooperatively fund and conduct R&D projects to fill key gaps in R&D/manufacturing infrastructure, such as developing new manufacturing processes and equipment, standards, and training programs.

SEMATECH remains one of the world's most successful industry-led R&D consortia, with significant experience in managing large-scale industry-government-university alliances. Our member-driven collaborative model and best practices are standard-bearers for industrial R&D consortia, and have been emulated and replicated both nationally and internationally.

SEMATECH is often cited as the model for successful public-private partnerships, based on our pioneering of the industrial R&D consortium model and our success in helping the U.S. semiconductor industry regain market share in the face of stiff competition from foreign competitors. SEMATECH has spurred both technology innovation and economic growth, including the creation of tens of thousands of high-wage jobs and billions in capital investment. SEMATECH is one of the few entities around the world that has continuously accelerated the RD&D timeline and delivered substantial value to its participants on an annual basis.

In our view, given the history of SEMATECH we have just described, several organizational features have been integral to the success of the SEMATECH industrial consortium model:

Commitment from senior executives, long-term support: Through their financial support, participation in programs, and assigned personnel, member companies make a substantial investment in SEMATECH, which in turn ensures that our activities are directly relevant to their needs and priorities.

Industry leadership: While SEMATECH was established as a public-private partnership, industry has retained the management lead, ensuring that the consortium's activities are aligned with industry priorities.

A clear, pre-competitive mission: SEMATECH accelerates commercialization by addressing common challenges, which are enumerated by the industry roadmap. This means a focus on building technology infrastructure and strengthening the manufacturing base.

Broad representation of the industry: SEMATECH engages the whole supply chain, including manufacturers, universities, national labs, research institutes, equipment/materials manufacturers and other suppliers. This engagement allows each entity to improve its understanding of its customers' needs, and helps drive alignment and consensus across the broader industry.

Leveraging of government and industry funds: Government funding does not displace industry funding; rather, it leverages it for the purpose of accelerating technology development. SEMATECH's initial federal funding of $100M per year was matched by industry, dollar for dollar. In the years that followed, the industry increased its share and SEMATECH became self-sufficient. This ongoing commitment is all the more notable in light of the tremendous financial pressures most national and international technology companies face.

A manufacturing development facility: The key here is scale. A shared facility where companies can practice manufacturing in a real-world manufacturing environment is a critical component, making it possible to test equipment, materials, processes and innovate new products at the scale that is necessary in order to demonstrate performance, reliability, and cost savings. Such a facility provides access to capabilities that enable next generation start-up companies to succeed and provide the critical validation of product performance for venture capital funding.

Membership model: SEMATECH is a member-driven organization. Participating companies provide technical personnel ("assignees") on two- or three-year rotations in addition to their financial contributions. Most immediately, this exchange of technical talent keeps SEMATECH attuned to member company priorities, but it is also is the critical means of transferring technology and manufacturing best practices.

SEMATECH has evolved over its 25-year history. In order to keep pace with and help lead a dynamic industry, it has expanded its program scope and its engagement with the supply chain, and diversified its funding sources. As a result, SEMATECH has:

- Helped recapture the US lead in semiconductor manufacturing,
- Successfully managed $870M in federal funding, ramping up membership, transitioning to self-sufficiency,
- Led industry-wide initiatives to enable industry transitions (next-generation patterning, next wafer size, novel materials and device structures), and
- Catalyzed technology commercialization and economic development.

APPLYING THE SEMATECH MODEL TO PHOTOVOLTAICS

At SEMATECH we see the incredible promise of renewable energy, and have already started to extend our experience in this direction, with the creation of the U.S. Photovoltaic Manufacturing Consortium (PVMC). Last year, the Department of Energy selected SEMATECH to establish the PVMC to accelerate the development, commercialization, and manufacturing of next generation solar photovoltaic (PV) systems. In keeping with the SEMATECH model, PVMC will provide a means for testing and demonstrating new technologies and manufacturing processes at production scale.

PVMC is leading a groundbreaking paradigm that will catalyze the 21st century solar PV industry, developing and commercializing innovations in renewable energy thin film technology to enhance performance and reliability while reducing the cost of manufacturing. This unique effort builds on the approach successfully demonstrated in the semiconductor industry, through the powerful combination of SEMATECH's collaborative industry consortium model and CNSE's public-private partnerships and unparalleled infrastructure.

PVMC private sector partners include companies from across the solar industry representing equipment, materials and metrology suppliers, module producers and integrators and end users. Working together with institutional partners, PVMC companies will provide the knowledge, experience and critical mass necessary to align the industry and propel it forward.

PVMC's goal is to increase the performance and speed the implementation of PV technologies while improving manufacturing processes and driving down costs. PVMC is working towards this goal by:

- Developing and disseminating technology roadmaps and standards in order to identify priorities and coordinate the technical agenda of the U.S. PV manufacturing industry,
- Establishing and supporting manufacturing development facilities to improve manufacturing productivity and increase U.S. PV manufacturing market share, jobs and technology innovation,
- Linking research labs, universities and industry to establish an effective PV commercialization support structure, and
- Developing a highly trained PV workforce.

Each of these strategic goals is supported by aggressive technical objectives, with detailed deliverables, metrics and milestones. Through its programs and advanced manufacturing development/prototyping facilities, PVMC will be a proving ground for innovative, disruptive solar technologies and manufacturing processes. Aligned and working together, the PV industry can overcome technology and manufacturing challenges, lower costs, regain market leadership, and spur the transition to a low-carbon renewable energy economy. Based on our decades of experience, we believe that this model of an industrial consortium working in partnership with universities and national labs can establish—or restore—national competitiveness in clean energy technologies.

INDUSTRIAL CONSORTIA: KEYS TO SUCCESS

SEMATECH was conceived by industry and government to stop and reverse the exodus of the semiconductor industry from the U.S.; the mission was ultimately successful, and SEMATECH has continued to evolve, adjusting to a dynamic industry and a dynamic world and economy, for the last quarter century. Our experience over that time tells us that the following are required to be successful:

- In any emerging/disruptive technology sector, a U.S. prototyping capability is needed to supplement R&D and bridge to manufacturing—that is, a manufacturing development facility (or facilities) that provides researchers and companies with the capability to test and prove out innovative technologies and manufacturing processes, either collaboratively or as part of a proprietary program or fee-for-service arrangement. This service goes well beyond what universities and national labs provide, with capabilities at sufficient scale to provide the data necessary to determine whether to adopt an innovation. A manufacturing development facility provides companies shared access to analytical, metrology, and advanced pilot line equipment required for integrating new materials, developing new equipment, and prototyping new products—services and manufacturing infrastructure not available in a lab environment.

- Collaboration with, and alignment of, a U.S. supply chain is needed to provide insight and guidance on the strategic investments required to achieve consortia goals; suppliers' direct engagement in collaborative R&D fosters innovation and accelerates progress toward commercialization. This is what Pisano and Shih have identified as the development of the industrial commons. ("Restoring American Competitiveness", HBR, July-August 2009)

- An efficient allocator of R&D funding is required—a consortium model provides a precompetitive mechanism to bring the industry together, prioritize and narrow technology options, reduce the risks of technology R&D, and maximize return on investment, to assure that funds are driven to productive applied research resulting in the acceleration of advanced manufacturing. It is difficult to evaluate long-term R&D programs, or adapt to rapid changes in technology. In these circumstances, the informed judgment of a combined cross-functional team of experts in a consortium is a better method of allocating R&D funding than a simple analytical model based on arbitrary assumptions when data or even reasonable estimates do not exist.

- A bridge between innovative research and funding/commercialization (e.g., across the Valley of Death) is needed, through a consortium model that spreads benefits/risk across all stakeholders, working with universities and national centers to pull critical research into the industry mainstream, working with industry to reduce costs/risks and accelerate precompetitive technology and process development, and working with government to realize the potential for economic benefit and job creation.

- Building and sustaining links to international partners is required. Industries are global; U.S. firms rely on global suppliers and have operations abroad, while many international firms make significant contributions to the development of U.S. innovation and manufacturing. While protecting our national interests and building our national technology and manufacturing capabilities, there are areas where international collaboration makes sense. To develop solutions that will be globally competitive, a consortium must have engagement with the global supply chain, especially in areas such as establishing common roadmaps, and providing access to critical materials and equipment sets. In particular, the issues of Environment, Health and Safety (EHS), standards, and quality/reliability are ones in which we all have a vested interest in establishing and maintaining a baseline standard. Ultimately, we have the know-how and methodologies to collaborate globally, while protecting national interests and protecting IP.

- The organization's success or failure rests on the integrity of the intellectual property management. A consortium must have an effective structure and methodology allowing collaborative, pre-competitive work while maintaining the integrity of the contribution of consortium members' IP and enabling the continuation into the competitive phase.

- A consortium is a collaborative effort that leverages resources; by combining both public and private resources, the consortium can expand the scope of its programs, investigate multiple technology options, and produce higher quality solutions, thereby multiplying many times over the undertaking that any single entity could afford.

- At the same time, the consortium must have a glide path to financial sustainability. We believe the membership model that draws member companies from all along the supply chain is critical to ensure that the consortium remains responsive to industry needs.

- A successful consortium must have the trust and confidence of the federal government, private corporations, and researchers/idea generators to provide the framework for, and realize the benefits of, our next generation of innovation-driven manufacturing. Trust and confidence comes from experience; the SEMATECH model has evolved with proven success in fostering technology innovation, reducing the costs of R&D, enabling advanced manufacturing, and creating high wage jobs and is respected worldwide.

CONCLUSION

In conclusion, we want to emphasize that for all of the challenges we face, we have faced similarly formidable challenges before, and we have the tools and the experience to overcome them. The Administration's National Network of Manufacturing Innovation holds a lot of promise in this regard. We believe that the NNMI can replicate SEMATECH's success across many industries, provided that it is guided by the core principle of industry management and that it utilizes the membership model.

The SEMATECH experience has reaffirmed that we as a nation can benefit from an ambitious national strategy to drive broad collaboration at sufficient scale to create technology roadmaps and standards; build R&D and manufacturing infrastructure; reduce cost across the supply chain; conduct both collaborative and proprietary technology programs; and provide access to pilot facilities to demonstrate innovations at manufacturing scale. In our view, public-private initiatives—that focus on investments that are too large for any single company or organization, and too long-term for companies that need to demonstrate quarterly results—are critical for the United States. In addition to leveraging our country's strong universities and venture capital system, we as a nation must nurture disruptive technology development and robust manufacturing, if we are to build the infrastructure for sustainable growth and leadership in the global economy. Given that the American taxpayer still funds the bulk of the underlying research, these activities return a significant ROI: in terms of generating revenue and high-value jobs, attracting companies to form a virtuous cycle of innovation-driven economic development, and thus enabling taxpayer-funded research to be commercialized here in the United States.

The CHAIRMAN. Thank you very much.
Dr. Scissors, please go right ahead.

STATEMENT OF DEREK SCISSORS, THE HERITAGE FOUNDATION

Mr. SCISSORS. Thank you.

I don't think we've heard enough today about how China is actually doing, and I'm going to say a few things about that, and maybe we'll hear more. I would also suggest or recommend to some extent my written testimony, which is hardly perfect, but documents a little bit on China's actual performance.

China's actual performance is poor. That I think is not really arguable. The reasons why, how long it will be poor, we can argue about, and those will imply some lessons for the U.S.

Let me start with positives on what China has done so far. They create jobs at home, partly by exporting solar panels, partly by having too much wind capacity for their own use. But jobs are good.

They also spend a lot, which makes it seem possible that there will be improvement in their future outcomes, which I think is fair—that possibility does exist—but that's it for the positives; and the negatives are pretty stark.

No. 1, China is now significantly more dependent on imported energy than it was. In 2007 China was a net coal exporter. It is now the world's largest coal importer, and it will pull away from everyone else in rather dramatic fashion.

Its oil important share is rising, so China is moving farther away from its stated goal of self-sufficiency that most countries have, including the PRC, and they're failing.

On efficiency gains, according to the International Energy Agency, in the decade of the 2000s U.S. energy efficiency improved annually at a 2.5 percentage point clip. China, which had far greater scope for improvement, much more room to improve, improved more slowly, 1.7 percent, percentage increase annually in energy efficiency.

They're not doing well in efficiency, either.

Ecology. We talk about green energy—we started talking about green energy primarily to reduce carbon emissions. In 2005 China was second to the United States in global carbon emissions. They have spent a great deal of money since. They are now at least 50 percent ahead of the U.S. in carbon emissions. That's the result of their green energy spending.

Innovation. Some people think that you spend money, you get more innovation. OK. I don't agree. There's very little primary innovation in China to this point. There's a lot of plans for innovation. Maybe we'll see it in the future. We haven't seen it yet.

Even in jobs performance, China's job performance in creating green energy jobs is heavily dependent on foreigners, particularly demand subsidies in the EU that are now drying up, or it's dependent on domestic overcapacity in wind.

So when we actually break down Chinese energy performance, it's bad. Why? Now we're moving into the suggestion phase. China extended a lot of support to large solar companies, for example. Let me give you a statistic. Three of the top 5—not all of them; 3 of the top 5—Chinese solar companies have debt now that is 6 times their market cap. The Chinese system has just failed, and those companies are either going to go out of business or just continually be subsidized by the State.

They try to innovate by decree: We will now innovate more. The decrees come a lot faster than protection of intellectual property. I would argue that, even with Chinese spending, if you don't protect intellectual property, which China is very far away from doing, you're not going to innovate, no matter how many orders you give from Beijing.

Their emissions profile changed when the State decided to alter the direction of economic policy, which was 2002–2003, a change in Chinese government. Their coal use was actually declining. Their coal use soars, their emissions profile soars, with a government change.

Their energy efficiency. China calls energy an area of absolute state dominance and it discourages competition because it wants to consolidate control of sectors on large state-owned enterprises. When you suppress competition, you get less efficiency.

China also imposes price controls. Price controls keep energy too cheap. They overuse it, they import it. There goes self-sufficiency.

The theme in all this is the state, the role of the state. That's my hypothesis for why China's energy performance is so poor.

So what are the implications for the U.S." Cooperation is certainly worthwhile. I think the current direction of China's energy policy is not going to accomplish anything. China's priority in energy is state control of energy, not technological breakthroughs, not reducing emissions. We've seen them do exactly the opposite.

I think imitating China is a terrible idea. They spend a little more than us and they get much worse results. Us imitating China would hurt the entire planet economically, environmentally, on any dimension you can think of, and it would cost us more, of course.

In the competition sense, we're winning. We're getting closer to self-sufficiency, they're getting farther away. Our energy efficiency is higher and we're gaining more. We're cutting our emissions, theirs are soaring. There's no sign of us losing our tech leadership, unless you just substitute "they're spending a lot of money, so eventually their going to pass us." Even in jobs, they spend a lot more money to create each green energy job and they may not be able to sustain their job performance to this point.

Now, is there anything we can do to do better? Of course there is. These are separate issues. I'm not arguing we're perfect. I'm arguing we're way ahead of China and we shouldn't lose track of that fact.

There was a brief moment of apparent bipartisan consensus on corporate tax reform. We need to go back to that brief moment. That would help us in green energy, energy, and everything else. I'm not arguing about the terms of that, just corporate tax reform I think both sides realize would be helpful. Some sort of agreement would be very helpful.

I agree with the chairman's opening comment entirely that a stable regulatory environment is very important and that jumping back and forth is not helpful. I would go on to add that I would prefer a minimally directive regulatory environment. Why? Because when you set out specific targets you pin us to technology paths that don't turn out to be the right ones. This is a very dynamic industry. We should not be looking and saying we know what technology should be chosen, we should subsidize it and that's the direction we're going to go in. We're going to be very sorry 5 to 10 years from now if we do that. So I want stability, but I don't want the government pushing industry in a certain direction.

Those would be my recommendations for the U.S., the main point still being that, let's not forget we're outperforming the Chinese in energy and by a wide margin.

Thank you.

[The prepared statement of Mr. Scissors follows:]

PREPARED STATEMENT OF DEREK SCISSORS, THE HERITAGE FOUNDATION

My name is Derek Scissors. I am Senior Research Fellow for Asia Economics at The Heritage Foundation. The views I express in this testimony are my own and should not be construed as representing any official position of The Heritage Foundation.

There are serious misconceptions regarding China's energy and environmental performance and what it means for the U.S. China is indeed spending a great deal of money on clean energy, but it is doing so largely in response to its own policy errors. The combined results of this spending and these errors are abysmal—waste, below-average gains in energy efficiency, lack of innovation, greater dependence on foreign sources, and a terrible record on the environment.

American misconceptions arise from the fact the Beijing has succeeded in one important area: green energy jobs. For the sake of jobs, Congress can choose to follow China's example, but the costs would be prohibitive. Not just money but efficiency, innovation, even environmental protection would have to suffer for the sake of employment. The U.S. boasts a far better energy and environmental record than China, and moving in China's direction would be very risky.

CHINA: IS GREEN ENERGY INVESTMENT HELPING?

One of the numbers that gets the most attention in clean energy debates is the amount countries are said to invest. According to the Pew Charitable Trusts, the People's Republic of China (PRC) spent a total of $100 billion in 2010 and 2011 on green energy, though noticeably less in 2011.[1] If "winning" in green energy is defined as just spending the most money, without reference to the outcomes, China is doing very well. That, however, is a very strange notion of success.

The first problem with grappling with how the PRC is actually doing is lack of transparency. Internal Chinese investment figures clash,[2] making it more difficult for foreign observers to draw conclusions. Some gaps are unintentional; elsewhere, there is deliberate obfuscation. China stopped publishing regular coal figures in 2010 as its share of global output approached 50 percent. It balks at almost any form of international monitoring, from a sweeping agreement on checking greenhouse emissions to U.S. embassy measurements of air pollution in Beijing.

A related problem is the contrast between capacity and actual use: The PRC's capacity to generate clean energy far outstrips its use. In wind power, the initial surge in capacity was half-wasted—over half the wind power generated in the first half of 2010 was unused. More recently, even capacity expansion in offshore wind has stalled due to delays and overcrowding.[3] In solar, Chinese equipment does get used, but almost entirely by others. The PRC now has the largest share of the world production market, but 95 percent has gone to exports.[4] China's world-leading investment in clean energy has managed not to provide the country with much clean energy.

Another area of the PRC's troubled "leadership" is hydropower. At home, hydro capacity outruns its use, just as with wind. Here the reason is not lack of connection but lack of water flow due to overconsumption and, to some extent, pollution. Major rivers now run dry and fail to reach the sea, and 25 percent of surface water is rated as unsafe.[5] Overseas, China has inked billions in contracts to build hydropower plants, mostly for less developed economies. These plants provide clear and important benefits but their environmental impact is dubious.[6]

COAL PRODUCTION (TONS, MILLIONS)

1998	1,110
1999	980
2000	880
2001	960
2002	1,110
2003	1,330
2004	1,610

[1] "Who's Winning the Clean Energy Race? G-20 Investment Powering Forward, 2011 Edition" Pew Charitable Trusts, 2012, http://www.pewtrusts.org/uploadedFiles/wwwpewtrustsorg/Reports/Clean Energy/Clean%20Energy%20Race%20Report%202012.pdf (accessed June 11, 2012).

[2] See the China Electricity Council cited in "China to See Slow Power Consumption Growth," Xinhua, February 7, 2012, http://www.china.org.cn/business/2012-02/07/content 24576241.htm (accessed June 11, 2012), versus the National Bureau of Statistics in National Bureau of Statistics, China Monthly Statistics, Beijing, Volume 1 2012.

[3] "Grid Issue Taking Wind Out of Energy Plan's Sails," China Daily, February 16, 2011, http://www.china.org.cn/2011-02/16/content 21933267.htm (accessed June 11, 2012), and Liu Yiyu, "Wind Firms in Doldrums," China Daily, May 31, 2012, http://www.chinadaily.com.cn/cndy/2012-05/31/content 15430337.htm (accessed June 11, 2012).

[4] "Factbox: How China Promotes Its Green Sector," Reuters, January 17, 2011, http://www.reuters.com/article/2011/01/17/us-solar-china-idUSTRE70G2CH20110117 (accessed June 11, 2012).

[5] Richard Spencer, "Yangtze River Water Level at 140-Year Low," The Telegraph, January 17, 2008, http://www.telegraph.co.uk/earth/earthnews/3322121/Yangtze-River-water-level-at-140-year-low.html (accessed June 11, 2012), and "China's Air Pollution Worsens After Economic Growth Rebounds From Crisis," Bloomberg, July 27, 2010, http://www.bloomberg.com/news/2010-07-27/china-s-air-pollution-worsens-after-economic-growth-rebounds-from-crisis.html (accessed June 11, 2012).

[6] Simon Marks, "Chinese Dam Project in Cambodia Raises Environmental Concerns," The New York Times, January 16, 2012, http://www.nytimes.com/2012/01/17/business/global/17iht-rbog-cam17.html?pagewanted=all (accessed June 11, 2012), and Derek Scissors, "China Global Investment Tracker Interactive Map," The Heritage Foundation, January 6, 2012, http://www.heritage.org/research/projects/china-global-investment-tracker-interactive-map.

COAL PRODUCTION (TONS, MILLIONS)—Continued

2005	1,820
2006	2,070
2007	2,290
2008	2,620
2009	2,960
2010	3,240
2011	3,520

Sources: National Bureau of Statistics, China Monthly Statistics, Beijing, Volume 1 1999—Volume 1 2010, and "Chinese Energy Chief Stresses Coal Consumption Control," Coal World, February 25, 2012, http://www.coalworld.net/indexnews/info.jsp?id=72651 (accessed June 11, 2012).

Notwithstanding all the green energy investment, coal dominates generation of both electricity and energy, and that dominance is not subsiding. On the (unreliable) official tally, energy consumption was said to rise 7 percent in 2011. Coal demand rose almost 10 percent so that its share in realized energy consumption expanded. Thermal power generation, which in the PRC is utterly dominated by coal, outpaced overall electricity generation last year because realized hydropower generation fell outright.[7]

This is not surprising; coal's role has waxed for over a decade, the very period where green energy is supposed to have become important. When hydropower is included, green energy has in fact receded while coal has advanced. In the late 1990's, coal accounted for a bit over 60 percent of the PRC's energy use and a bit over 70 percent of its electricity. Those numbers are now 70 percent and 80 percent, respectively. Coal use accelerated most noticeably starting in 2002-2003, when the current Chinese government took office and emphasized investment in power-intensive heavy industries such as steel.[8] Eventually, supply could not keep up. As recently as 2007, China was a net coal exporter; it is now the world's largest coal importer.[9]

STATE DOMINANCE AND ITS IMPACT

For a decade, the economic model has been to lend, invest, produce, and export. Coal and other energy consumption has essentially been forced to rise in response, far more than if growth had been consumption-or services-led. A simple way to understand Chinese energy investment is the state trying to clean up after itself. It typically fails because Beijing simultaneously takes actions that limit the value of clean energy investment.

The government does not encourage or shape energy development; it dictates it. The State Council requires "absolute control" of all energy production, starting with price-setting. When prices are permitted to rise, subsidies are often offered as compensation, so government involvement still increases. Price controls have consistently caused production of natural gas to fall short of grandiose plans.[10]

But coal, as usual, provides the starkest example of double-sided, self-defeating government intervention. Effective price controls, through electricity prices and central government coercion, keep coal cheap for industrial expansion and lead to more coal use.[11] This prompts calls for clean energy. But the subsidies Beijing then pro-

---

[7] "China Energy Consumption Rises At Fastest Pace in Four Years," Bloomberg, February 22, 2012, http://www.bloomberg.com/news/2012-02-22/china-energy-consumption-rises-at-fastest-pace-in-four-years.html (accessed June 11, 2012), and National Bureau of Statistics, China Monthly Statistics, Beijing, Volume 1 2012.

[8] Derek Scissors, "Deng Undone: The Costs of Halting Market Reform in China," Foreign Affairs, May/June 2009, http://www.foreignaffairs.com/articles/64947/derek-scissors/deng-undone (accessed June 11, 2012).

[9] "China Surpasses Japan As Largest Coal Importer," Dow Jones, January 25, 2012, http://www.iss-shipping.com/microsites/NewsDetails.aspx?msid=194&newsid=6439 (accessed June 11, 2012).

[10] As an illustration, see "Chinese Cities Grappling with Natural Gas Shortage," Xinhua, November 23, 2009, http://english.people.com.cn/90001/90778/90860/6821411.html (accessed June 11, 2012), and "Australia Cancels $40.4 Billion Natural Gas Contract with China," People's Daily Online, January 5, 2010, http://english.people.com.cn/90001/90778/90860/6859711.html (accessed June 11, 2012).

[11] "Development and Reform Commission Asked for Breach of Contract Prices of Coal Enterprises to Resume Contract Price," Xinhua, June 25, 2010, http://www.china-daily.org/China-

vides to green energy to make it competitive are much larger than they would have to be if the price of coal was not kept too low in the first place.

Beyond prices, the latest incarnation of state energy policy is the 12th five-year plan. Some goals, such as those for electric vehicles, are far from being met.[12] Others are standing orders modified only by placing the word "new" before the word "energy." One such goal is to suppress competition. The three national oil majors account for well over 90 percent of oil production and over 95 percent of gas production. Oil and solar may seem strange bedfellows, but the PRC is molding solar in oil's image, handing out gigantic loans to a select few solar companies and then implementing regulations on standards that will drive most small firms out of business.[13]

The PRC spends heavily on green energy in large part because it has bigger energy and environmental problems than any other country in the world. Most of those problems are inflicted by the Chinese state itself. Giving Beijing credit for spending on green energy is like looking at a stunt driver's medical bills and giving her credit for investing so much in her health.

STATE CONTROL OF ENERGY—A SUMMARY

Coal	Price controls discourage use of other sources
Gas	Price controls discourage competition, innovation
Oil	Regional monopoly blocks competition, innovation
Solar	Trying to imitate oil

CHINA AND THE U.S.: WIN OR LOSE

Sino-American energy and environmental relations can be cooperative, competitive, or imitative. Most observers would choose cooperative, but a country that fights transparency and adopts contradictory policies is not a pleasant partner. Joint research, touted in the Strategic and Economic Dialogue, is reasonable, but expectations should be minimal. Beijing's clear pattern is to put state control of energy first, with energy efficiency and ecological protection secondary.

In this light, any breakthroughs would come from the U.S. and then be adopted by China. This is occurring now in natural gas, where China is openly jealous of American progress. The PRC is said to have larger shale reserves than the U.S., but its huge, sheltered companies and massive spending have seen it only fall further behind in technology and extraction, and Beijing has been forced to seek foreign assistance.[14] Cooperation with China should be seen more as a contribution to the global community than as a way to make progress on American aims.

Competition: We Win

If the PRC does get help to tap its gas reserves, it will of course become a competitor for the U.S. This has already happened in wind, solar, and elsewhere: China took technologies developed by others and became a major commercial presence. Is this an economic or energy threat to the U.S.? It depends first on American priorities. For more than a generation, the U.S. has emphasized energy efficiency and innovation while seeking self-sufficiency and trying to protect the environment. This approach has borne fruit.

If the top priority is energy self-sufficiency, Chinese actions are not directly relevant to the U.S. However, the extent of American self-reliance has been increasing

News/Development-and-Reform-Commission-asked-for-breach-of-contract-prices-of-coal-enter-prises-to-resume-contract-price/ (accessed June 11, 2012).
[12] "China 'Can Still Lead' in Green Cars," China Daily, April 21, 2012, http://www.china.org.cn/environment/2012-04/21/content 25200574.htm (accessed June 11, 2012).
[13] "Yingli's $5.3b Loan May Help China Double Global Solar Panel Supply," China Daily, July 9, 2010, http://www.chinadaily.com.cn/business/2010-07/09/content—10087488.htm (accessed June 11, 2012), and Du Juan, "Solar Industry 12th Five-Year Plan Issued," China Daily, February 25, 2012, http://www.china.org.cn/business/2012-02/25/content_24728487.htm (accessed June 11, 2012).
[14] "China's Shale Reserves Already Surpass the U.S.," Real Clear Energy, December 19, 2011, http://www.realclearenergy.org/charticles/2011/12/19/chi-nas_shale_resources_already_surpass_the_us.html (accessed June 11, 2012), and Leslie Hook, "China Sets Target for Shale Gas Development," Financial Times, March 16, 2012, http://www.ft.com/intl/cms/s/0/2e7a77ac-6f59-11e1-9c57-00144feab49a.html#axzz1xQ5FoJl0 (accessed June 11, 2012).

while China's decreases, so that the PRC's model provides little reason for a change in American policy.[15]

AMERICA VERSUS CHINA: THE SCOREBOARD

TARGET	WINNER
Self-sufficiency	U.S.
Efficiency	U.S.
Ecology	U.S.
Technology	U.S.
Jobs	PRC

If the top priority is energy efficiency, the U.S. is clearly winning. Poor data from Beijing again obscure the situation, but China's economy was half the size of the American economy by the end of 2011. Yet the Energy Information Administration, which has consistently underestimated the PRC's expansion, estimates its energy consumption at 10 percent-15 percent larger than American energy consumption last year. The efficiency gap has been widening. The International Energy Agency found the U.S. improved energy efficiency 2.5 percent annually from 2000 to 2009, compared to China's 1.7 percent. This occurred despite the much larger scope for improvement on the western side of the Pacific.[16]

It is difficult to imagine true competition in technology in the foreseeable future. The PRC has a huge market and will continue to try to lure foreign players to offset its own failings, but the requisite state control of energy and lack of protection for intellectual property are powerful disincentives. It is not surprising that the larger energy investments have been made by Chinese firms in the U.S., rather than the reverse, led by gas but also including biofuels and wind.[17]

If the top priority is a cleaner environment, there is no competition: Cheap Chinese solar panels, wind turbines, or natural gas all contribute positively to that end in all countries. In fact, they seem to contribute more positively to protecting the environment outside China than inside.

Cleaner energy improves water and air quality, both areas where America far outperforms China, but attention has been focused on capping or reducing greenhouse gas emissions. The record shows the U.S. as the world's best performer since 2006, the golden age for green energy.[18] The PRC, in stark contrast, has moved from roughly equal to the U.S. in emissions in 2006 to half again higher or more (with an economy half the size). China's emissions per unit of GDP are thus four times America's and its emissions per capita, while lower, are soaring. Projections over the next decade have gross Chinese emissions larger than the rest of the world combined.[19]

---

[15] "BP Energy Outlook 2030," BP, January 2012, http://www.bp.com/liveassets/bp_internet/globalbp/STAGING/global_assets/downloads/O/2012_2030_energy_outlook_booklet.pdf (accessed June 11, 2012).

[16] "International Energy Outlook 2011," U.S. Energy Information Administration, September 2011, http://205.254.135.7/forecasts/ieo/pdf/0484(2011).pdf (accessed June 11, 2012), and "China Passes U.S. as World's Biggest Energy Consumer," Bloomberg, July 20, 2010, http://www.businessweek.com/news/2010-07-20/china-passes-u-s-as-world-s-biggest-energy-consumer.html (accessed June 11, 2012).

[17] Ryan Dezember and James T. Areddy, "China Foothold in U.S. Energy," The Wall Street Journal, March 6, 2012, http://online.wsj.com/article/SB10001424052970204883304577223083067806776.html (accessed June 11, 2012); "China Egg Producer to Set Up U.S. Biogas Project with Smithfield," Bloomberg, February 17, 2012, http://www.bloomberg.com/news/2012-02-17/china-egg-producer-to-set-up-u-s-biogas-project-with-smithfield.html (accessed June 11, 2012);, and Brian Spegele, "Chinese Firm to Build Big Wind Farm in U.S.," The Wall Street Journal, September 20, 2011, http://online.wsj.com/article/SB10001424053111904106704576579741179230646.html (accessed June 11, 2012).

[18] "Global Carbon-Dioxide Emissions Increase by 1.0 Gt in 2011 to Record High," International Energy Agency, May 24, 2012, http://iea.org/newsroomandevents/news/2012/may/name,27216,en.html (accessed June 11, 2012).

[19] Justin Gillis, "Carbon Emissions Show Biggest Jump Ever Recorded," The New York Times, December 4, 2011, http://www.nytimes.com/2011/12/05/science/earth/record-jump-in-emissions-in-2010-study-finds.html (accessed June 11, 2012), and Keith Bradsher, "China Fears Consumer Impact on Global Warming," The New York Times, July 4, 2010, http://www.nytimes.com/2010/07/05/business/global/05warm.html (accessed June 11, 2012).

EMISSIONS TREND (TONS, BILLIONS)

Year	U.S.	PRC
1998	5.65	3.65
1999	5.69	3.57
2000	5.87	3.56
2001	5.75	3.64
2002	5.82	3.92
2003	5.87	4.50
2004	5.94	5.28
2005	5.94	5.85
2006	5.84	6.50
2007	5.91	7.01
2008	5.46	7.78
2009	5.04	8.11
2010	5.25	8.95

Source: Jos GJ. Olivier, Greet Janssens-Maenhout, Jeroen A.H.W. Peters, and Julian Wilson, "Long-Term Trend in Global CO_2 Emissions: 2011 Report," PBL Netherlands Environmental Assessment Agency and Institute for Environment and Sustainability (IES) of the European Commission's Joint Research Centre (JRC), 2011, http://www.pbl.nl/sites/default/files/cms/publicaties/CO_2%20Mondiaal_%20webdef_19sept.pdf (accessed June 11, 2012).

The final priority is jobs. The reason Beijing ratcheted up lending, investment, and production in 2002-2003, thus ratcheting up coal use and carbon emissions, was to create jobs. Renewables are more labor-intensive than fossil fuels, sometimes far more.[20] This is a drawback from the standpoint of cost and efficiency but a positive with regard to employment. A natural result is that a job-seeking China will favor green energy more than an efficiency-seeking U.S. will.

Further, when domestic supply outruns demand, the excess is shipped overseas. Chinese jobs then seem to come at the expense of foreign jobs, a source of broader tension. In energy, solar is the most obvious example: Chinese solar subsidies are wildly excessive if the purpose is just to serve the home market; they began as a response to incentives offered in Europe. With Europe now unable to afford its incentives, Chinese panels have been diverted to the U.S.

Imitation: We Lose

As in other areas, the U.S. is suffering in clean energy from China's job-seeking. Should America fight fire with fire? Should Washington even go beyond simple retaliation and adopt "the Beijing model" in energy? Should Congress pass legislation aimed at China that would create more green energy jobs in the U.S.? The short answer to all three questions is "No." Jobs would be created but at the cost of a pronounced deterioration in overall energy performance.

If green energy was already as efficient as conventional, no subsidies would be needed. More green energy jobs at the moment means less energy efficiency. Further, truly ensuring job creation requires picking winners. Small, nimble firms can drive large employers out of business: Jobs first means this competition must be suppressed, as in the PRC. The result is unavoidably less innovation. Finally, more clean energy jobs means less clean energy. Chinese subsidies harm U.S. manufac-

[20] Robert Pollin, James Heintz, and Heidi Garrett-Peltier, "The Economic Benefits of Investing in Clean Energy," Department of Economics and Political Economy Research Institute (PERI), University of Massachusetts, Amherst, and Center for American Progress, June 2009, http://www.peri.umass.edu/fileadmin/pdf/other_publication_types/green_economics/economic_benefits/economic_benefits.PDF (accessed June 11, 2012).

turing but cut the price of power generation from renewables. Blocking Chinese goods would raise the price, make green energy less competitive, and undercut ecological gains.

The worst idea, though, is for America to imitate China in clean energy. Even if Beijing were making wise choices for China, it is extremely unlikely these choices would be wise for the U.S. The U.S. is in a far better situation than China. The U.S. has a fundamentally more conducive system for innovation. The U.S. would certainly suffer from imitating Chinese practices with regard to transparency.

The U.S. is also blessed with a far better resource endowment—more usable land and much more water per person. The water gap, in particular, is an obstacle to Chinese natural gas development. So it is no surprise that China invests a good deal in water. But it would still make no sense at all for the U.S. to match this investment. Coal generates about twice as much of America's electricity as natural gas does. Coal generates about 20 times as much of the PRC's electricity as natural gas does.[21] This is not a model that the U.S. should follow.

Even in solar, subject of much debate, the end of European incentives reveal the cost of Chinese subsidies. As a group, LDK Solar, Suntech Power, and Yingli Green Energy were offered tens of billions in government assistance, and their announced debt runs in the billions. Their combined market capitalization is now short of $1 billion. U.S. government solar subsidies can be deemed inadequate compared to China's, but the same is true for ensuing losses. All the PRC has on its side is raw spending, spending that is often wasted and other times is merely an attempt to compensate for harmful policy decisions in other spheres. The U.S. has done far better.

The CHAIRMAN. Thank you very much.

Let me start with a few questions. This analogy to what was done with Sematech I think is an intriguing one. My recollection of that experience was that the industry itself, the semiconductor firms themselves, Bob Noyce and others, came to Washington and basically said: We need to do this, we want to do this, we need government assistance to help us get started, and we did that.

At the same time, my recollection is that the original members of Sematech were U.S. companies. I think NEC applied for membership and was not permitted to be a member at that time, was my recollection.

I guess what I'm now sort of struggling with is, if there were to be consortia of companies to pursue their competitive position in some of these technologies in photovoltaics or other areas, how do we go about identifying that organization? Is there a critical mass of industry that want it that are U.S.-based or that have operations in the United States, that would want to do such a thing? I guess those are some obvious questions.

Mr. Wolff, do you have thoughts on it?

Mr. WOLFF. Just to begin, and I'm sure Mr. Holladay has some current thoughts on the subject, Sematech was industry-driven, you're quite right. Bob Noyce and the other, IBM, ATT, both the vertically integrated companies and the Silicon Valley companies, Texas Instruments as well, found that they were not as efficient or producing as good a production as the Japanese. It's one thing to say, well, there's dumping. It's another thing to say, we don't have the quality that the others do. We needed to drive our manufacturing efficiency, our toolmaking, our processes, and the way to do that was in a hands-on laboratory environment that actually was a factory that produced something, not for commercial use, but to learn how to make better chips.

---

[21] Frank Wolak and Richard Morse, "China's Green Gift to the World," The Guardian, December 30, 2010, http://www.stanford.edu/group/fwolak/cgi-bin/sites/default/files/files/China's%20green%20gift%20to%20the%20world__Dec%202010__Wolak_Morse.pdf (accessed June 11, 2012).

You're right that this was a U.S. effort entirely. It was funded by the Department of Defense, $100 million a year, as has been testified to, for 5 years, and the industry also matched that with a $100 million contribution. So it was a major effort, and it paid off.

The industry has become global. There are foreign participants in Sematech today and they're still pushing the envelope, and it's all pre-competitive R and D, and the benefits for the world have been dramatic in terms of the information revolution.

Whether there's enough of a consensus in the U.S. private sector today I would leave to the person who's currently involved with them in the Sematech initiative with respect to photovoltaics.

The CHAIRMAN. Mr. Holladay, what's your take on whether there's a critical mass of industry interested in anything comparable to Sematech or any kind of collaboration to improve their competitiveness?

Mr. HOLLADAY. Yes, sir, especially in the supply chain. The supply chain is really desperate to be able to have, especially access. The manufacturing development facility is critical. Having a facility where people can do, not lab-related work, but they can actually go do production-related work and develop production-style tools and test production materials, and it's critical to the supply chain to be able to develop these more advanced materials, these more advanced tools, and having access to those kind of facilities?

The CHAIRMAN. That's what you said you have been tasked to do or are working with the Department of Energy to do? Did I understand that.

Mr. HOLLADAY. Yes, sir, in the SIGs, in some crystalline silicon areas. So we have a very great opportunity. It's the first time that Sematech's been replicated in 25 years, and the Department of Energy has created that aground the SIGs technology and, like I said, some components of the crystalline silicon, and we're working to expand that.

The CHAIRMAN. It strikes me that, at least for several of you, this point about maintaining in the U.S. a manufacturing capacity has been made, and that the ability of the U.S. to remain a leader in research and development is not going to be possible if we don't have that manufacturing capacity in these technologies. I just wondered if anybody wanted to elaborate on that. Mr. Prestowitz, you made that point, I believe.

Mr. PRESTOWITZ. Yes, I did. I think it's an important point. I think there's a false sense widely spread that innovation proceeds in kind of a straight line, that you do basic R and D in a laboratory someplace and then that proceeds to developmental R and D that proceeds to commercialization. That's not really how it works. It's an iterative process.

It's very often that somebody in the field comes up with an idea that they throw at the lab and back and forth. If you don't have the bach and forth capability, much more difficult to do the innovation.

I think that we've seen that in so many instances that this concept of past dependence, that what happens next depends on what happened the step before, and if you don't have the step before then the next step doesn't happen, is pretty solidly established both economically and scientifically. That's the point, I think.

The CHAIRMAN. Mr. Holladay, did you want to add something?

Mr. HOLLADAY. I agree with that 100 percent. I'll add to it just a little bit. A great deal of innovations happen on the shop floor or they understand the innovation to be able to pull it from the research side. If you don't have the manufacturing side to really understand the innovations or pull them from the research or have an industry pull and a market pull mechanism, then you lack that innovation.

The other thing is, you need to know how to integrate that innovation into the manufacturing line. As you lose the manufacturing, you lose those opportunities.

The CHAIRMAN. Mr. Wolff.

Mr. WOLFF. There's a wonderful book called "Bell Lab: The Idea Factory" that you may have read, by John Gertner, that came out this year, and it was engineers and basic scientists who were creating fabulous inventions, driven by industry and driven by the need to actually have practical manufacturing outcomes, including ultimately the transistor, which of course gave birth to, through Bob Noyce and others, to the integrated circuit.

So we don't have a Bell Labs today other than what DOE and a Sematech can do. Those are our current idea factories.

The CHAIRMAN. Senator Murkowski.

Senator MURKOWSKI. Thank you, Mr. Chairman.

I suggested in my opening that the United States was doing relatively well in this race. Dr. Scissors, you seem to agree with me. Some of the others are suggesting that China is ahead.

I guess the question to you would be whether or not it is constructive to even talk about this being a race for the clean energy title. Is it fair, is it constructive, to say that we are in a race? Then if it is so, if it is appropriate to refer to this as some kind of a competition, which everyone has used that word, and we all recognize that words matter here, but if this is a competition what's the metric that we use?

How do we judge who's winning and who's losing? Is it a question of how much money has been deployed? Is it the generating capacity that is then put in place? Is it a calculation of reduction in emissions? How do we even measure this to know who's up, who's down? I throw this out to all of you because I think it is an important part to this discussion. Is it all about how much money is spent or is it the outcome at the end?

Mr. Wolff.

Mr. WOLFF. If it's a race to deploy clean technologies then it's a very useful thing to do. We ought to both be successful in it. China needs to do more, for reasons of environment and to change their energy sourcing.

Are there places to collaborate? I think so, with respect to carbon sequestration, clean coal technology, perhaps in PV, perhaps some things in wind.

I am struck by the fact that in consumer electronics Japanese industrial policies took us out and we've come back. We came back with iPhones and iPads, at least on the invention side, and a lot of the benefit is to our economy.

But you don't know that you're going to come back, and here the bet is not about consumer products like consumer electronics, but whether we can have within our economy the ability to generate not only the R and D and the invention, but commercialization, and I think that's important.

Senator MURKOWSKI. Let me ask, and maybe this will give better definition to the others: Is it about just deploying it, making sure that you've got the wind turbine up, but if that wind turbine isn't connected to anything, if it's not generating, is that something then that says China is more successful in deploying this?

Again, what are these metrics? Mr. Wu? I'll just go down the line here.

Mr. WU. Thank you for your question. I think, Senator, I think that's a very good point, and it's difficult for us to say there's one metric. There's many ways of measuring it. But if we may offer one suggestion, it's grid parity that matters. It's being able to——

Senator MURKOWSKI. Grid parity?

Mr. WU. Grid parity, being able to deploy clean energy at a cost-effective, sort of cost-effective way that is competitive with fossil fuels and other forms of energy.

So I think it's not about how many turbines you put up every year if they don't work. It's about whether or not you can do that in a cost-effective way and you can produce energy from it that's also cost-effective for consumers and also cost-effective for the economy.

Senator MURKOWSKI. Others? Mr. Prestowitz.

Mr. PRESTOWITZ. I think to some extent I sense a little bit of cross-talk here when we say we're doing better than the Chinese. If we're talking in terms of reducing emissions, I think that's right. The U.S. is doing better than China in reducing emissions. We have had a great boom from shale gas, and thank God we've had it, and so that's been a big piece of our reduction of emissions, and we've also benefited from rising gas mileage in automobiles and so forth, conservation measures, again, very positive.

But that's a little bit different than the question we're talking about. I mean, you may also want, in addition to reducing emissions by dint of shale gas, you may also want to have the potential to reduce emissions by dint of solar, solar photovoltaics or wind power or battery-driven technologies. If you do want that or if you think that those technologies also have potential new knock-on capabilities for the future and you want that for the future, then you need to question how you're doing in that. Then your metrics, how you're doing in that, are, well, how much is being invested, what's the state of your technology versus the other technology, what is the rate of deployment, what's the rate of innovation. These are all pretty measurable things.

The measurements that we have so far seem to indicate that the Chinese and others—again, I don't want to just put this on the Chinese, but the Koreans, Japanese, Taiwanese, Germans, many others—have advanced fairly rapidly and in many instances more rapidly than we.

You ask, are we in competition? I have to say yes. These industries are characterized by economies of scale and by imperfect competition. They're not win-win industries. They tend to be zero-sum industries. That is, when one's winning somebody else is losing. Typically the aircraft industries or auto industries or any major capital-intensive industry. In those kinds of industries, if you're not keeping up in investment and in R and D, then typically you're falling behind. That seems to be the trend that the U.S. has found itself in, not an irreversible trend.

Senator MURKOWSKI. My time has expired, but I've got two more that I'd like to hear from if they will. Thank you.

Mr. Holladay or Dr. Scissors.

Mr. HOLLADAY. I guess the best way for me to describe what the late great Nobel Laureate Dr. Smalley discovered before he passed away and spent a lot of time looking at: If you can find a solution to energy, you have a solution to many of the top ten problems humanity faces over the next 50 years. So there's a lot of reasons that we need to address clean energy, find solutions to energy—national security, diverse fuel mixes.

Right now, photovoltaics, for example, is in the early stages of its life cycle. Its bright future is still to come. The technologies being developed today are not the technologies that will actually be deployed in a wide level in the upcoming years. But we will come to that point. It's going to be a huge market globally. So it's critical that the United States be a leader in that of next generation technologies and that we position ourselves to do that.

Senator MURKOWSKI. Dr. Scissors.

Mr. SCISSORS. I know what metric we shouldn't use, which is how much money we spend. I think most people would say spending more money is bad unless you get something for it, and the Chinese aren't. So we want to save money. We want to spend as little as possible and do as well as possible. So the idea that somebody spending more money than you is a good thing doesn't make any sense to me.

When you look at how they're actually performing, why did we start with clean energy? We started because we're concerned about carbon emissions. It's not something to just dismiss and way, well, that doesn't matter now. It does matter, and the U.S. is doing pretty well and China is doing terribly. That's a metric. It's not the only one, but it's one.

Energy efficiency I mentioned before. We're doing better than they are in energy efficiency. We're doing better than they are in self-sufficiency.

So different people, different members of the committee and of the Congress, are going to have different metrics. Money should not be the metric. We want to see what we're getting for what we're putting into this. Gas is an excellent example. The Chinese are extremely jealous of gas extraction in the U.S. They don't have the technology for it; we do. So who's winning the innovation battle? We just won the biggest innovation battle of the last few years in clean energy. Are we going to lose the next one? It's possible. We're not doing perfectly. But the amount of money we're spending is not the way to measure the outcome.

The CHAIRMAN. Senator Wyden.

Senator WYDEN. Thank you, Mr. Chairman. I think this has been an excellent hearing, very good witnesses.

Let me start by saying, I think the principal question for our panel and for our challenge in the days ahead is how our country is going to respond to what has been described by some experts as China's green mercantilism? There is a new paper* out this morning, Mr. Chairman. I would just ask unanimous consent to put it into the record. They, in the paper, define "green mercantilism" as essentially policies that give other countries an unfair advantage in terms of our interests, allow them to boost their exports, limit imports of clean energy technologies.

Mr. Wolff, for me you really summed it up when you said in your testimony—you asked essentially, is it acceptable for Chinese industrial policy to shape the U.S. economy? I think that that sort of incorporates the essence of this issue with respect to green mercantilism, and it also goes beyond the trade issue, which I think is important for us. I also chair the Finance Subcommittee on International Trade. I'm interested in expanding trade. I don't think free trade means trade free from rules.

What is appealing to me about the way you asked it, it gives us a chance to shape the challenge, both in terms of trade and other kinds of issues.

So why don't we start with the other 4 witnesses responding to Mr. Wolff's question. His question was: Is it acceptable for China's industrial policy to shape the U.S. economy? Give me your response to his question and, if you think it is unacceptable for China to be shaping our policy, what do you think we ought to do in a proactive way to combat it? Let's start with you, Mr. Wu.

Mr. WU. Thank you for the question. No, I don't think it's acceptable. I think the point that also Senator Murkowski brought up earlier is whether or not we should emulate China. I think the answer to that is also no.

The fact of the matter is the economies of the United States and China are different, and the reality is also that China has a vast amount of energy demand that's still growing and they have a very high reliance on coal at the moment, and that's a very different situation to what we have here in the United States. I think I agree with what Dr. Scissors mentioned earlier about sort of the gas, the question about gas, which is, yes, I think China is looking a little bit with envy over to the United States regarding our ability to export shale gas, which China does have vast reserves of, but currently lacks the technology to exploit it on the level that we have done here in the United States.

So I think the answer is no, we have to take a very different look at the way the economies of the United States and China are.

Finally, I would just like to add that, with regards to metrics, yes, I think China has done very well in what it's done very well, which is manufacturing. China makes a lot of things, not just clean energy goods. So it has exploited its advantage, which is to manufacture solar PV and also wind turbines on a very large scale, and has done so in a very cost-effective manner, which we can argue whether it's good or bad for who and for whom. But also one perhaps benefit of that is that it's been able to reduce the cost of re-

---

*Document titled "Green Mercantilism: Threat to the Clean Energy Economy" has been retained in committee files and can also be found at http://www.itif.org/publications/green-mercantilism-threat-clean-energy-economy.

newable energy significantly, at least for China, for its domestic consumption.

Senator WYDEN. Mr. Prestowitz, I know that you don't think it's acceptable for China's industrial policy to shape the U.S. economy. What do you think our country should do in a proactive way to combat it?

Mr. PRESTOWITZ. I think we have to use our heads. I don't think that it's acceptable for China to shape our economy, but at the same time I don't think that we need willy-nilly to imitate everything that China does.

As Derek points out, everything that China does is not necessarily right.

So I think what's required us for us to spend some time thinking hard about what is it that's really important to us, and then take the measures that are necessary to counter the negative impact on us achieving our goals of some of these mercantilist policies. So for example, we know that an element, an aspect of the mercantilist policies tends to be excess investment in the promoting country, followed by dumping.

Typically in the U.S., we wait for an affected company or entity to file an antidumping complaint before we do anything about dumping. We don't have to. The Secretary of Commerce has the authority to self-initiate antidumping cases. So one thing that I've advocated is, let's monitor industries where other countries have active, proactive industrial policies, look at the extent of their overinvestment and their dumping activity, and self-initiate cases, take them to the WTO right away, preempt them. That's one element.

Typically, such countries have currency manipulation policies. Typically—not just China. Singapore, Taiwan, Korea. They intervene in currency markets every day to keep their currencies undervalued. Take measures to counter that. Impose capital controls if necessary. Tim Geithner can do it, doesn't even have to ask the Congress for permission.

Set up consortia, a la Sematech or PV Tech or whatever it is. I think that a big factor in the United States is investment taxes. I think that very often the incentives for investment in the United States are not nearly as attractive as they are for investment abroad. Singapore is the world champion at attracting foreign investment. We could learn well to copy a lot of what Singapore does.

So it's a matter of what's important to us, all right, then what's our strategy, and a combination of carrots and sticks to get what's important for us.

One point, and just to emphasize what Alan said, is this. Typically, I know Alan and I have been involved in some of these discussions for a long time. Typically, you get into these debates in the administration, whoever's administration, and the argument is we don't pick winners and losers and we shouldn't be intervening to subsidize or provide corporate benefits. What's lost in that discussion is that in a situation in which you're facing an active industrial policy abroad, a decision not to intervene is a decision. A decision not to pick winners and losers is a decision to pick a loser. You're not going to be in that industry. That I think doesn't get understood today.

Senator WYDEN. I know my time is up. If we could just, Mr. Holladay and Dr. Scissors, again responding to the question Mr. Wolff said.

Mr. HOLLADAY. No, sir, I don't think we should dictate our international policy, but we do need to be focused, we need to have vision, we need to understand where our country's going and where the global technologies and market are going, so that we can be strong and successful. To build on the not picking winners and losers, the consortium model is perfect for that. You pick the technologies, you have a collaborative model where you don't just spread the dollars around, you better leverage our universities and our national labs to really impact the industry, and it's critical that we do that.

Senator WYDEN. Dr. Scissors.

Mr. SCISSORS. I have one objection to the green mercantilism designation. The word "green" is unnecessary. They're mercantilist and they're big, which means we cannot avoid Chinese industrial policy affecting the U.S. economy. We don't like it, but it's true.

To me the best response is to get them to do less of it. We're not going to get them to stop, and that should include threatening them. There are things China doesn't want to give up and we need to push them to try to get their industrial policy to back off in certain areas.

Where that isn't going to work, sometimes their subsidies help us. They make things cheaper here for American consumers. Sometimes they hurt in ways we can't respond to. So I think my colleagues on the panel have all said a variation of the same thing: We need to identify not everywhere they affect us, no avoiding it, but where we don't like them affecting us and where we can respond properly. That's a subset. So we need to focus down and say, all right, here's the big group of things, where can we do something that's useful that really matters.

Senator WYDEN. Thank you, Mr. Chairman.

The CHAIRMAN. Let me ask another question. One of the frustrations I have had is that we don't seem to have a willingness to do on the procurement, government procurement side, what other countries do on a regular basis. For example, China is not a signatory to the government procurement agreement under WTO, so they're not obligated to give fair opportunity to foreign producers of products that they might buy through their governmental organizations.

Should we be doing more with buy-America policies to try to support U.S. industry? I mean, I'll give you a specific. I attended the groundbreaking ceremony last year in Santa Fe and the photovoltaic cells, of course, were made in China. We make photovoltaic cells even in New Mexico and we make them in other parts of the country, but the Chinese cells I'm sure were cheaper and they were purchased by the contractor who was hired by the governmental agency that was putting in the photovoltaic panels.

Should we be doing more to urge that U.S. Government and U.S. governmental entities pursue a buy-America policy when it comes to U.S. industry? Mr. Wolff?

Mr. WOLFF. I think that the fact that, in the case of, again it was semiconductors in the very early stages, transistors and then semiconductors, government demand initially drove the startup of this industry. Government demand started titanium. Government demand in the manned spaceflight program really gave us our start on nanotechnologies. Government demand gave us an Internet. Government demand gave us new materials and GPS.

So intelligent use of government demand is I think a very important component of national policy. It has to be balanced against cost. We're not interested, I think, in having an inefficient procurement system. But it can't be only cost. It has to be maintaining a domestic base as well.

The military is a major consumer and has a major interest in, for example, in renewables, with targets to increase the amount of renewable energy that's sourced, for both national security and cost reasons. I think that that program is a very important one that has to be considered with respect to its support of the U.S. industrial base.

The CHAIRMAN. All right.

Mr. Prestowitz.

Mr. PRESTOWITZ. Just a point on cost as well. I recently drove over the new—the Oakland Bay Bridge in California, which is still being built. You know, the main spans of the bridge are being made in China, and the reason for that is because initially the Chinese had a very low bid on the steel fabrication for those main spans. It turns out that they're way behind schedule and way over cost, and California is not only not saving any money, but it's also not generating the jobs it might have generated had it actually procured the bridge in the United States.

The CHAIRMAN. Senator Murkowski, go right ahead.

Senator MURKOWSKI. Thank you, Mr. Chairman.

This kind of follows onto the chairman's question. I think we recognize that oftentimes if we have a buy-America requirement that that may add to the cost. I appreciate you noting that sensitivity, that we've got to balance that.

Another area where we may be adding to cost is when we put in place Federal requirements or mandates for production of renewable fuels, whether it's through Federal or State renewable energy standards, clean energy standards. The President has proposed a new Federal mandate for clean energy, the CES. The chairman has been working on some legislation.

But I think we recognize that, in an effort to comply with these requirements, sometimes those—the equipment that the utilities will turn to will be American-made, other times it will not be American-made. We've got tensions between the goal of environmental improvement on the one hand and then job creation here in this country on the other hand.

Is this a situation where ultimately we're going to be able to figure this out and we really are able to have our cake and eat it too? Or will we invariably be dealing with a situation where we have to prioritize one over the other? It's either going to be more affordable energy, but maybe we compromise on whether it is built here in America with jobs in America, or a tradeoff with environmental aspect?

Do you see us getting to a point where it really is U.S. jobs, it really is a win when it comes to reduced emissions, and truly being able to have it all? Do we get to that point, or are we constantly in this point of tension and prioritization of one over the other?

Dr. Scissors.

Mr. SCISSORS. I think unfortunately we're constantly in this tension. Unless the U.S. without subsidies, which of course cost money and raise the effective cost of the clean energy, is the superior provider across the whole range of whatever clean energy technologies we're using at the time, which is very, very unlikely, then somebody else is going to be making something more affordably than we are, for whatever reason, including industrial policy, subsidies, however they're doing it.

So then we have this choice. Do we want the very heavily subsidized Chinese solar panels that are cheaper and will make solar more competitive within the U.S. market and provide us with affordable clean energy, or do we want to say, they subsidized those things and that cost American jobs and we don't want to do that? It's not an easy choice. I don't mean to be suggesting that for a second. I mean that unless the U.S. private sector alone, because if you spend government money that counts as the cost of energy, beats everybody else, some foreign technology is going to be useful for helping our environment and providing affordable clean energy. When we use that foreign technology, we don't make it here.

So there's just no way to escape this. It's a tough choice and we're stuck with it.

Senator MURKOWSKI. We'll go down here, Mr. Wu and then Mr. Wolff.

Mr. WU. Thank you. I would respectfully slightly disagree with that. I think it's not—to add a little more nuance, I don't think it's a stark choice. The idea—energy is a very localized resource. It's about energy security. You're putting in a wind turbine or a coal plant or a nuclear plant, it's located in one location, which if it's providing energy to the United States it has to be located in the United States. Therefore, it can generate jobs for maintenance, for installation, for the ongoing operation of the plant over many, many years.

We know that a lot of the jobs and economic benefits of solar and wind, in addition to also traditional energy, is generated with where it is located, which is the maintenance of the wind far, installation of solar panels, and et cetera.

So I think it's not to say that none of this will be manufactured -all of it will be manufactured in the U.S. and none of it comes from China. There will be a mix. So I think there is a little more nuance to just one or the other, it all comes from one location or it all has to be based in another location.

Thank you.

Senator MURKOWSKI. Mr. Wolff.

Mr. WOLFF. I think the purpose, one of the purposes, of the government backing joint research and development and a strategy including trade policy and other policies is to drive down the cost of whatever we're trying to affect. In semiconductors we did get an agreement with Japan not to sell below average cost of production by company. The net result was that Korea and Taiwan came on stream in memory chips and the United States remained in that kind of technology, and Micron Technologies—with no continuing

50

trade relief. That's gone 15 to 20 years ago. But Micron Technologies is one of the most competitive companies in the world, out of Boise, Idaho, and bought facilities in Japan and produced there as well, because the Japanese market was totally open.

So I think that the net result has to be not only to have the technologies continue to be developed here, but to drive costs down a learning curve. We've been very successful with that in a number of areas, and my suspicion is that the Sematech photovoltaics is going to achieve that as well.

Senator MURKOWSKI. Mr. Chairman, thank you.

I appreciate the comments from the witnesses and the time they've given the committee this morning.

The CHAIRMAN. Thank you.

Let me just ask another question or two. Senator Franken has sent us word that he's anxious to ask a few questions and he's on his way back from the Capitol. So let me ask a question or two while he's on his way.

I guess one obvious question is, if a semiconductor—or a Sematech-like entity is created with regard to photovoltaics or any of the other clean energy sectors, how does that translate into us actually manufacturing those products here? Frankly, my impression is that we don't have enough U.S. firms to make a Sematech-like entity on photovoltaics right now. We would have to have a more global organization, and if we did why would that manufacturing not be performed elsewhere?

Mr. Holladay.

Mr. HOLLADAY. Yes, sir. When you create this type of hub, this manufacturing development facility, it creates a catalyst. It brings in the equipment suppliers, it grows new companies, it gives companies the opportunity—it gives you business advantages that don't exist anywhere else in the world potentially unless, like Fromhoffer, who kind of replicated the Sematech model for their energy piece.

But what it does is it brings the industry in. There's a lot of industry anxious. They know for photovoltaics, for example, that that's going to be a huge market. So industry grows around that and, like with Sematech, it creates hundreds of thousands of jobs. A supply industry comes. You're able to develop next generation technologies and it just creates this catalyst that grows the industry around this infrastructure that you've established, this production infrastructure that does not exist in the lab-scale environments of the universities and most national labs.

The CHAIRMAN. Senator Franken, I advised folks that I was filibustering until you returned.

Senator FRANKEN. Go ahead, Mr. Chairman.

The CHAIRMAN. No, no.

Senator FRANKEN. No, no.

The CHAIRMAN. I have asked my questions and we're now anxious to hear what questions you have. Thank you.

Senator FRANKEN. OK. Thank you.

Mr. Wu, Mr. Prestowitz, I'd like to give you an opportunity to respond to some of Dr. Scissors' testimony, because it struck me that some of the statistics that he was citing or using, such as China's increased reliance on oil and coal and its lack of energy efficiency improvement vis a vis or compared to the United States, that they're a function of its growing economy. I think that without that context that testimony was kind of—it just needed that context, because otherwise it's kind of meaningless.

I just want to have you put it in context for me. While China was expanding its economy, I think in some years in double digits, and in 2007–2008, I think the last quarter of the Bush presidency, we cratered to a negative 9 percent of GDP, well, of course we're going to be using less energy and being less reliant on coal and oil.

So can you comment on that?

Mr. PRESTOWITZ. Yes. I think you're right. In fact, I think the Chinese, it seems to me, are actually to be admired in a way in this. Obviously, they're trying to maintain the high growth, the 8 and 9 and 10 percent growth rate, and that for them has been very energy intensive, and it's been very energy intensive with the worst kind of energy. They've got the worst kind of coal and they've kind of got the worst kind of oil. If you travel to China, you travel in a total miasmic haze and everybody has a cough, and the Chinese are aware that that's not good.

So it's precisely because of that that they've put such emphasis on trying to develop alternative sources. They've been catholic about the alternative sources, looking at all possibilities. So I think that the fact that China's emissions are worse than ours and trending worse than ours doesn't take away from the significance, importance, and their commitment to alternative energies.

So then the question becomes, well, in the alternative energy field are they performing—are they doing dumb things? Are they investing in the wrong technologies? Are they doing smarter things? It's a mixed bag. They're probably overinvesting because the incentives to invest have been made very attractive. Essentially, the party has told the regional banks to lend. This is like the old days in Japan where the MITI told the banks, lend, and so they lent.

But that then gets to this question of, OK, maybe they're overinvesting and maybe we wouldn't do it that way. But that then begins to impact on us, and so you then get to the question of are these technologies, put aside the coal and so forth, but are the technologies that the Chinese are pursuing—and again I want to emphasize, it's not just China. Japan, Korea, Taiwan, Singapore, Denmark, Germany, all of these guys are in the game. So are those technologies silly, we should forget about them and just concentrate on fracking in the U.S. Or are those things that could be important for the U.S."

If they're important for the U.S.—I believe they are, long-term—then we need to have a strategy to maintain viability technologically and commercially.

Senator FRANKEN. Mr. Wu.

Am I going to get a little bit more than 5 minutes here?

The CHAIRMAN. You take whatever time you'd like.

Senator FRANKEN. OK, thank you.

The CHAIRMAN. Certainly.

Mr. WU. Thank you, Senator. I completely agree with that, and I agree with what Dr. Scissors said earlier as well. I think all the metrics are true. The emissions have grown, energy efficiency—or energy intensity, rather, has gotten worse. Over 70 percent of China's primary energy use comes from the industry, heavy industry and manufacturing, which is very intensive in terms of energy consumption.

So I think that it's good that you point out, Senator, the context of this, which is we're looking at sort of massive economic growth and also energy use growth. Also, I think, as Mr. Prestowitz said earlier, sort of the effort is also important as well. If this investment in clean energy or if this deployment in clean energy were not to take place, what would it be? I would say probably right now it has not so far not made as much difference as perhaps the Chinese government hoped. The power generated from wind, the massive wind deployment in China, is quite a bit lower than what we see in the United States or also in Europe.

So if you look at the recent 5-year plans and also——

Senator FRANKEN. Is that the amount of wind or the use of the wind energy it's created, because it sounds like some of it's being not put to use?

Mr. WU. It's both. It's the efficiency of the ones that are operating and the total amount, the total percentage of ones installed versus ones that are working. So you have three-fourths of it which are turning and then the other quarter which are not turning, and then of the ones that are turning the efficiency is a lot lower.

So if you look at the recent 5-year plans, the policy, the idea is to turn that around, to increase the technology, to increase the efficiency. I think a lot of expertise has to actually come from ultimately European engineers, which are going to China and being hired by Chinese companies in very large numbers, to help turn this around.

So I think in terms of what we want in the United States, yes, the quality versus quantity is do we want to emulate the massive manufacturing scale that we see in China and produce as many wind turbines and solar modules as possible, or do we want cheap, affordable clean energy that's higher efficiency, that is actually going to be part of our energy mix in the future? So I think that's probably the more important question we should consider, which is why I brought up the idea of grid parity earlier, which is renewable energy that is competitive with other energy sources. Perhaps that is one metric or one goal that we should be thinking about.

Mr. SCISSORS. Senator, can I just make one small point of context for your context?

Senator FRANKEN. Absolutely.

Mr. SCISSORS. Thank you. I appreciate that. It will be very short.

I take your point. I just want to bring up one thing. From 1998 to 2002 China was growing fine and their coal use was shrinking. So it isn't just that they're growing and they're using more energy, as my colleague just suggested.

They're growing in a certain way that's using a lot more energy and a lot more kinds of energy, and that is swamping the other things that they're also trying to do. So that's probably a more refined way of saying—I accept your correction—what I should have said in my introduction.

Senator FRANKEN. Mr. Wolff, or Ambassador Wolff.

53

Mr. WOLFF. If I could add just one element, and that is it would be great if China had 15 times the amount of clean energy that they have deployed now. We're not in that sort of race, it seems to me. When a State in the U.S. adopts a clean energy standard, it really isn't doing it because of trade considerations. However, what the Chinese have done is, as Mr. Wu has just testified, they have not deployed the best windmills in the world, the best wind turbines, which come from Vestas, a Danish company, Sezlon, an Indian company, General Electric, a U.S. company.

They've kept us all out, and they buy the cheapest turbines, but not cheapest in terms of their productivity in terms of generating electricity on a sustainable basis over a significant amount of time. So I wouldn't—as a metric, I'm not concerned with their use of deploying a great deal of renewables. We ought to do it, they ought to do it. That's I think—our only concern is that we breathe the same air around the world and it would be nice if they had more clean energy. But we do care about being kept out of their market and we do care about them depressing our production here, our industry that can produce this equipment.

Senator FRANKEN. By flooding or just by keeping us out, or both?

Mr. WOLFF. Both.

Senator FRANKEN. OK.

You mentioned clean energy standard and a State adopting that. Minnesota adopted at the time the highest renewable energy standard for utilities in the country. It was 25 by 25 was the goal. XL Energy, our largest utility, was charged to going to 35, I believe, by 2025, and they're ahead of the goal of achieving it.

There's different ways to go at this, but it seems to me—and the chairman has produced a clean energy standard piece of legislation—that adopting a national clean energy standard would be something that would incentivize the creation of clean energy and renewables. I'd like to have a renewable energy standard within the clean energy standard, something that would incentivize these industries.

Does anyone disagree with that? Dr. Scissors.

Mr. SCISSORS. Why would you think it would be me? I think you actually touched on where I would disagree with it in exactly what you just said. You moved from clean to renewable, and I'm going to say that I would want, if you impose a standard like that to incentivize industries, the definition of "clean" to be as broad as possible. I don't mean that you include everything. I mean the broader it is, the more chance you have for industry to pick the right technology path, not to be bound to what we think today is the good renewable energy and the productive renewable energy and the one we're going to be using 10 years from now.

Senator FRANKEN. But there are a lot of renewable energy——

Mr. SCISSORS. Right, exactly. There are also some clean—I agree with that. There are also some clean energies that people would not count as renewable. If the goal is purely to be clean, then let's just be clean. We're not in danger. If the goal is we're worried about running out of something, then we have to change the standards.

My advice to the Congress first would always be, be as broad and non-specific as possible.

Senator FRANKEN. So your issue with me is the renewable part, not the clean part?

Mr. SCISSORS. My issue with you is the slipping of that definition, where the narrower the definition becomes the worse the outcome's going to be, because we're going to be pushing people toward a smaller and smaller range of choices.

Senator FRANKEN. I just think that in Minnesota we did it renewable and it's worked out really well in many, many ways. In Minnesota, we have manufacturers in Minnesota creating solar panels. We have very good things happening. Actually, it promotes diversity, which is I think what you're talking about, not tieing ourselves to—if you call nuclear clean energy and you call natural gas clean energy and you call clean coal with some sequestration clean energy, we can get a clean energy standard without going to any renewables whatsoever.

I think that if we're going to create diversity, which I think is what you're talking about, let a thousand energy flowers bloom, I think that putting some renewable in there is a good idea.

Mr. Scissors, you did say we shouldn't be subsidizing industry. I was taken with something before I had to leave, with what Mr. Prestowitz says, which is that very often there isn't like this—I think what you said was, there isn't just this straight line where you start developing a technology and it starts here and then you employ people like that. It seems like, I think what Mr. Prestowitz was saying, is that there's a fallow period in terms of job creation and then it kicks up.

In semiconductors, Sematech, it sounds like it started and then it worked and it took off. How many people were employed by the Internet during the first 10 years of its development at DARPA? Just the people at DARPA. How many people employed by the Internet now? Gee, a lot of people.

So it seems like—how many people were employed by the space industry when our rockets—when I was a kid, our first rockets went [indicating]. Remember those? We're coming to you by CSPAN, the Cable Satellite Public Affairs Network. This is telecommunications. That was started by the government. But that didn't create a lot of jobs in the beginning. No one knew exactly what that would yield. But all our telecommunications, all our GPS, everything comes from that.

So this idea that, OK, well, these aren't creating jobs right now—these industries will create. Our clean energy technology has to create jobs. I mean, I believe it will create millions and millions and millions of jobs in the future. It's creating jobs now, too.

But the idea that just because it's not creating jobs now and that we don't have to subsidize industries—we've subsidized so many successful industries in this country that it's hard to think of—it's hard to think of one that didn't enjoy a government subsidy. The Erie Canal sort of brought the Midwest to Europe so we could ship our agricultural products and our timber to Europe, so we could get to the Hudson River and so we could get to New York. That was a government investment.

So this idea that we shouldn't choose winners or losers and we shouldn't subsidize industries that have the potential to employ millions and millions of people and to better our lives, Look at the nuclear industry. We were just talking about nuclear as one of the clean energy standards. Where would that be without the Manhattan Project? Where would that be without the Tennessee Valley Authority? Where would that be?

So I think that we have to be very careful when we look back at our actual history. I've heard some of my colleagues on the other side, not today of course, say that this should all be free enterprise, there's no role for the government in this stuff. There has been a role for the government in this stuff.

I know that sounded like a speech, not a question. But I was kind of wrapping up.

The CHAIRMAN. Most questions around here sound like speeches.

[Laughter.]

The CHAIRMAN. Let me thank the panel. This was very useful testimony, a very useful hearing. We appreciate it very much, and that will conclude our hearing.

[Whereupon, at 11:18 a.m., the hearing was adjourned.]

[The following statement was received for the record.]

STATEMENT OF RHONE RESCH, PRESIDENT & CEO, SOLAR ENERGY INDUSTRIES ASSOCIATION

Chairman Bingaman, Ranking Member Murkowski and members of the committee:

The Solar Energy Industries Association (SEIA) is the national trade association for the U.S. solar energy industry. On behalf of our 1,000 member companies and the more than 100,000 American taxpayers employed by the solar industry, I appreciate having the opportunity to submit a statement for the record on the important topic of China and clean energy.

According to a United Nations report released earlier this week, global investment in renewable energy reached a record $257 billion in 2011, with solar energy attracting more than half at $147 billion. This represents a year on year increase of 52%, led by strong demand in Europe, China and here in the U.S. These trends are indicative of a rapidly evolving, highly competitive and robust global industry.

The strong growth of the solar industry, however, has coincided with increased competitive pressures throughout the solar value chain. While SEIA supports the ability of sovereign nations to implement policy designed to promote the production and use of renewable energy, these incentives must be consistent with international trade rules and the obligations of our trading partners.

AMERICA AND THE GLOBAL SOLAR VALUE CHAIN

Solar cell and module production are important parts of the solar manufacturing process. It is, however, important to note that U.S. manufacturing in the global solar value chain extends beyond these stages in the production process. Today, there are at least 95 domestic facilities in 26 states manufacturing photovoltaic ("PV") primary components, including solar-grade polysilicon, ingots, wafers, cells, solar modules and inverters. Only 19 of these facilities were operating in 2005—a five-fold increase in the U.S. in the last six years. These products are not only utilized domestically, but are also destined for growing export markets.

For example, Hemlock Semiconductor employs 900 workers at their Michigan plant that processes silicon feedstock, an essential component in solar panels. The company is currently building a facility in Clarksville, Tennessee which is expected to employ another 500 workers. The construction workforce to build the facility already tops 1,600 people.

In addition, a number of companies manufacture inverters domestically. Inverters are a key component in a solar energy system; they turn the direct current produced by a PV panel into the alternating current that is used by lights and appliances. For example, Siemens Industry, Inc. employs 100 people at its inverter manufacturing location in Alpharetta, Georgia. Among its many solar products, DuPont Photovoltaic Solutions manufactures solar film at its Circleville, Ohio facility. Sixty-three Ohioans produce this high value solar film, which is then used in PV panels installed across Europe and North America. These are just a few examples of U.S. companies that rely on access to markets at home and abroad to sell their products and create jobs here in the U.S. Overall, 73% of the value of an installed PV solar system is domestic.

As with other industries, trade disputes will emerge as a market becomes competitive and global in scale. The agreements set forth through the World Trade Organization ("WTO") attempt to clarify what are acceptable forms of support and what options countries have to counteract unfair practices that are inconsistent with WTO-rules. SEIA supports the rules-based global trading system and the use of enforcement mechanisms, such as anti-dumping and countervailing duty litigation, when appropriate. Litigation is a vital aspect of maintaining free and fair global trade flows, and SEIA supports the right of countries to investigate unfair trade practices and address them accordingly.

RESOLUTION OF GLOBAL TRADE DISPUTES

Litigation and trade remedy measures, however, should be employed judiciously. More importantly, litigation and trade remedies are not the only avenue for pursuing an equitable and robust global solar marketplace that benefits both U.S. manufacturers and consumers.

Equally essential to the global trading system are dialogue and negotiations. Averting escalating trade disputes is in the interest of manufacturers in the domestic solar value chain that want access to growing foreign markets and U.S. consumers who benefit from the reduced energy costs that come with an efficient and competitive marketplace from solar products.

Towards this end, SEIA is working with national solar trade associations from around the world to create a public-private dialogue on solar trade and competitiveness issues, beginning with the creation of a Clean Energy Partnership within the Asia-Pacific Economic Cooperation ("APEC"). Such a forum would provide an opportunity to help clarify the role of government in encouraging the development of national solar industries and, in turn, improve the competitive landscape for U.S. companies, both within the U.S. and abroad.

The initial goals of an APEC Clean Energy Partnership would be to:

• Promote WTO-acceptable trade in solar energy goods, while taking into account the role of governments in the development of the solar energy industry;
• Ensure that global innovation, scaling and economic development occur; and
• Create a collaborative framework for preventing trade conflict in the solar industry and resolving it constructively if conflict does arise.

Building on successful collaboration within the private sector, the American and Chinese governments should also begin working together towards a mutually-satisfactory resolution of the growing trade conflict within in the solar industry.

LOCAL CONTENT REQUIREMENTS

Open markets and the free flow of products within the confines of the rules-based trading system will continue to drive down costs for consumers and help significantly expand the deployment of solar technology in America. Conversely, the imposition of requirements that solar energy products utilized in a particular market be domestically produced, commonly referred to as local content requirements, should be avoided. These requirements generally run afoul of WTO rules and incite the imposition of retaliatory market barriers. This in turn would lead to costly inefficiencies in the marketplace.

As nations around the world recognize the energy policy benefits associated with the deployment of solar technology, there has been a growth in trade-distorting local content measures. For example, solar programs in Ontario, Canada and India feature local content requirements which preclude American companies from competing in these promising markets. To prevent the expansion of such provisions and rollback existing policies, SEIA is building upon its collaboration with other national solar trade associations to create a multilateral, public-private forum focused exclusively on local content provisions. One potential outcome of such a forum could be the development of a list of WTO-consistent best practices that could serve as alternatives to local content requirements. In this context, SEIA also encourages U.S. policymakers to avoid imposing local content requirements on domestic solar incentives.

THE U.S. NEEDS SMART, STABLE POLICY TO CONTINUE GROWTH IN THE DOMESTIC MARKET

Access to a diverse, abundant, reliable and affordable supply of energy is in the national interest. Accordingly, federal policy has for decades provided a legislative and regulatory framework that has helped every major source of energy utilized in the U.S. today reach commercial scale. The recognition that smart policy can play a vital role in developing new domestic energy resources has contributed significantly to America's long-term economic prosperity and growth.

Similarly, history has shown that well-crafted and efficient federal tax incentives can be powerful policy mechanisms to promote the nation's energy objectives and leverage private sector investment for the deployment and utilization of new energy resources. This is clearly the case with federal tax incentives designed to promote the expanded deployment and use of solar energy technologies.

Since the enactment of the 30 percent commercial and residential solar Investment Tax Credit ("ITC") in 2005 and the 1603 Treasury Program ("1603") in 2009, domestic deployment of solar has increased seven-fold; the cost to consumers has significantly dropped; and we have developed a domestic industry value chain that today employs over 100,000 Americans. By any objective measure, these important incentives are doing exactly what they were meant to do—allow our nation to reap the significant energy, economic and environmental benefits associated with utilizing our abundant solar resources.

When compared to other sources of energy—both conventional and renewable—the duration of federal support for solar has been brief. The solar ITC is the primary federal policy that encourages the deployment of solar technology. Since the ITC took effect in 2006, the industry has made significant and concrete strides towards grid parity. If current trends continue and costs continue to drop on account of economies of scale, improved technology and enhanced efficiencies, the solar industry's need for federal policy support will be shorter than virtually any other domestic energy source.

Ultimately, it is the entrepreneurs in America's solar industry—from the scientists developing more efficient and cost-effective solar technologies to the market innovators providing new financing options that make solar more affordable for consumers—who are responsible for the rapid growth and reduced costs that are the hallmarks of America's solar industry. Stable, reliable and well-structured tax policy provides the framework that allows for this market-driven innovation. If policymakers have the foresight to retain these highly effective tax policies, this short-term investment will yield significant long-term benefits.

CONCLUSION

Chairman Bingaman, Ranking Member Murkowski and members of the committee, SEIA again appreciates having the opportunity to submit a statement for the record on this important hearing on China and clean energy. A national policy that recognizes the benefits of open markets, both at home and abroad, combined with smart and stable domestic policy will accelerate the deployment of solar technology, continue the positive trends of reduced costs for consumers and create jobs throughout the solar value chain. SEIA looks forward to working constructively with you to achieve these worthwhile policy outcomes.

APPENDIX

RESPONSES TO ADDITIONAL QUESTIONS

RESPONSES OF DAN W. HOLLADAY TO QUESTIONS FROM SENATOR MURKOWSKI

Question 1. How significant is the role played by the cost and availability of energy in the United States' competitive position, compared to China's?

Answer. Cost and availability of energy will become one of the most significant problems facing humanity in the next few decades. As the demand for energy becomes the limiting factor for growing economies and sustaining basic needs, being a leader in the manufacturing of affordable clean energy will position any nation for a more independent, economically stable future. The cost of energy is a critical component of the cost of doing business, but the business environment in China is beyond the purview of SEMATECH's expertise.

Question 2. How would each of you define the term "green job"—or do you think we should even have a separate category for them—and do you think "green jobs" are any more or less susceptible to outsourcing than regular jobs?

Answer. The debate over green jobs is complex and encompasses issues of economic competitiveness, national security, and climate change. The issue of outsourcing, however, is more straightforward, and doesn't necessarily involve sending jobs overseas. For example, companies routinely outsource administrative functions such as event planning and payroll, but those functions don't necessarily move offshore. The Committee is quite rightly concerned about the larger issue of offshoring, as it potentially denies the American taxpayer the return on investments in research. As a nation, we have come to realize that favoring research over production removes critical manufacturing "know-how" from the iterative process of innovation; many of the most impactful innovative breakthroughs come from the collective knowledge developed on the manufacturing shop floor. Eventually, research follows manufacturing leaving U.S. companies without the business, and the nation dependent on foreign suppliers.

SEMATECH's experience is grounded in an established industry in semiconductors, which has provided capabilities and spin-off technologies for numerous emerging industries (nano-biomedical, MEMS/NEMS devices, nano-materials, energy harvesting and generation, etc.), all of which provide technology leadership, generate economic wealth and thus enhance our national competitiveness. Although, through the DOE's leadership, SEMATECH has most recently championed sustainability programs that are aimed at solar energy manufacturing and deployment, thus reducing industry's environmental footprint, we would argue that rather than focusing on just on what's "green," our policy focus should be owning the leading edge of technology. When we develop technology responsibly, and own the leading edge, our industries retain competitive advantage and our nation maintains a strategic advantage.

RESPONSES OF DAN W. HOLLADAY TO QUESTIONS FROM SENATOR CANTWELL

U.S.-CHINA TRADE RELATIONS

Question 1. Do you agree that there is much more to gain for both the US and China from a cooperative framework on our mutual clean energy interests?

Question 2. How would the witnesses characterize the extent of overlapping interests within the American and Chinese markets for clean energy?

Question 3. Could eliminating tariffs and non-tariff barriers to trade in clean energy and environmental goods and services be beneficial to both countries?

Question 4. What particular mechanisms can we use to eliminate existing tariffs and non-tariff barriers on clean energy technologies?

Question 5. Do you believe that the final result of these recent trade cases will be good for our clean energy industries as a whole?

Question 6. Do escalating trade complaints on all sides endanger growth, investments, and jobs in emerging clean energy industries?

Question 7. In terms of our international competitiveness going forward, what sort of incentives are in place in China to promote clean energy development and deployment and how do they compare to the U.S. from your perspective?

Answer. Trade policy is not within the purview of SEMATECH's organizational charter, but we strongly advocate the benefits of collaboration across the national supply chain, and selective international collaboration where it makes sense, as an effective complement to trade policies. We have seen, through SEMATECH's experience as a national consortium, the power of creative cooperation to align and achieve national interests. Today we are an international organization, and today's leading industries are global. U.S. firms rely on global suppliers and have operations abroad, while many international firms make significant contributions to the development of U.S. innovation and manufacturing. We believe there are areas where international collaboration is both possible, appropriate, and critical to the overall success of an industry, while protecting national interests and building domestic manufacturing capabilities. Our position has been that an industrial consortium must have engagement with the global supply chain in order to develop solutions that will be globally competitive. This is especially evident in areas such as establishing common roadmaps, providing access to critical materials and developing common standards and protocols. More specifically, for example, we all have a vested interest in establishing and maintaining a baseline for Environment, Health and Safety (EHS) standards. Ultimately, we have the know-how and methodologies to collaborate globally, while protecting national interests and protecting IP.

POLICY ENVIRONMENT

Question 8. Do you believe that if we fail to create the right policies and investment incentives at home, we'll miss out on lucrative opportunities for global leadership in clean energy?

Answer. Yes. The U.S. is no longer acting alone on the global stage, as one might argue it did in the 1960s. In today's competitive global economy, the investments that are not made here are made elsewhere and the resulting economic benefits accrue to others. There is a danger that the U.S. can be reduced to a producer of intellectual property that is ultimately commercialized elsewhere. This economic outcome denies the American economy the tremendous economic benefit that comes with transforming IP into products—both revenues and jobs—and ultimately denies the American taxpayer a return on the investments in the underlying research. Public-private partnerships such as SEMATECH can be instrumental in preserving—or establishing—U.S. leadership in critical industries, including many clean technologies. Our member-driven collaborative model and manufacturing best practices are standard-bearers for industrial R&D consortia, and have been emulated and replicated both nationally and internationally. After twenty-five years of operation, SEMATECH is one of the few entities around the world that has continuously accelerated the RD&D timeline and delivered substantial value to its participants on an annual basis, with our focus on filling key gaps in the R&D/manufacturing infrastructure, developing key tools, materials, and processes, and providing testbed facilities to demonstrate and evaluate innovations in a production environment.

TAX POLICY

Question 9. Wouldn't placing a clear price on carbon be one of the policies that would spur our clean energy industries?

Question 10. Assuming comprehensive tax reform is not happening this year, will jobs be lost if we fail to extend these expiring credits that industries have been banking on?

Question 11. On the flip side, will businesses create jobs if these provisions are extended for a predictable period of time?

Question 12. As Congress begins to grapple with a major reform of the tax code, would you be willing to trade the certainty of multiyear extensions for a sunset date for all energy tax subsidies?

Question 13. Do you think it's fair that some energy sources benefit from permanent subsidies and others have to deal with the uncertainty of short-term extensions?

Answer. Tax policy is outside the purview of SEMATECH's organizational scope of expertise. As a general matter, we do believe that the tax code should not choose among technologies, but rather should be framed in terms of desired outcomes. This approach invites the market to develop innovative solutions to meet policy objectives.

R&D BUDGETS

Question 14. If securing our energy independence, averting climate change and creating new energy industries and jobs are true national priorities, shouldn't our energy R&D budgets be more on the scale of NIH?

Answer. A strong commitment to R&D and manufacturing is critical to the growth of our economy and the health of our industrial base. Consistent and substantial investments in life sciences research have yielded world-class pharmaceuticals and medical devices. A comparable commitment to the physical sciences is critical if we are to continue to see the breakthroughs that will unleash energy savings in existing industries and create entirely new ones. Equally important, the U.S. is no longer acting alone on the global stage. In today's competitive global economy, the investments that are not made here are made elsewhere and the resulting economic benefits accrue to others.

ROLE OF THE DEFENSE DEPARTMENT

Question 15. Do you believe that the Department of Defense can play an important role in facilitating our emerging domestic biofuels industry?

Question 16. Would these efforts advance our national security, both by decreasing our energy dependence and by reducing our military's expenditures on the full costs of energy over the long term?

Answer. SEMATECH does not have any programs in the development of biofuels per se. Our experience, however, does illustrate the important and positive role that the Department of Defense can plan in cultivating and maintaining a robust industrial base. As the Committee knows, SEMATECH originated with the Defense Department's need for semiconductor devices and manufacturing equipment. The public-private partnership that ensued yielded much more than a secure supply of critical components for the Defense Department; indeed, working collaboratively, the industry has facilitated breakthroughs in new devices and materials that have revolutionized data processing and communications.

RESPONSES OF ALAN WM. WOLFF TO QUESTIONS FROM SENATOR MURKOWSKI

ENERGY COSTS AS A FACTOR OF COMPETITIVENESS

Question 1. For all the talk of China's advances in clean energy manufacturing, the country is struggling mightily with environmental challenges. China has long since passed the United States in total greenhouse gas emissions and approximately one quarter of its water resources have been deemed unsafe. As I mentioned in my opening statement, the country's solar panel factories don't tend to run on solar power. The unfortunate irony of all this is that America has often relied upon the cheaper, dirtier manufacturing practices of China in order to affordably comply with requirements we've imposed on ourselves for cleaner, pricier energy here at home.

How significant is the role played by the cost and availability of energy in the United States' competitive position, compared to China's?

Answer. It is clear that the new techniques to extract gas from U.S. rock formations will greatly enhance U.S. competitiveness as a base from which to produce goods. Whether this changes the competitive relationship with manufacturing in China depends on many factors—relative exchange rates, relative rates of inflation, relative costs of capital, relative productivity gains, relative wage levels, as well as how successful the U.S. and China are in lowering energy costs. Clearly the competitive relationship will be improved with the lowering of energy costs in the United States, all other things being equal.

DEFINITION AND OUTSOURCING OF GREEN JOBS

Question 2. There was a bit of renewed interest in "green jobs" recently, when an administration witness testified that this category of employment includes everything from college professors and antique dealers to bicycle repair clerks and used record shop employees. In addition to these broad definitions, others have said that green jobs "can never be outsourced." Together, these claims have created a lot of confusion about - and, frankly, mistrust of - the pitches that have been made in support of stimulus spending and other activities.

How would each of you define the term "green job" - or do you think we should even have a separate category for them - and do you think "green jobs" are any more or less susceptible to outsourcing than regular jobs?

Answer. By far the largest category of jobs that will be stimulated by increasingly changing the mix of energy to renewable sources will be those in deploying the solar and wind equipment. The second largest category is likely to be those jobs involved in production, assuming that the equipment is produced onshore. A third category will be the engineers, scientists, and administrative personnel involved in the industry. The first and last of these groups are not very susceptible to our-sourcing—namely deployment, and at present, invention (the front end of innovation). What we are not assured of at present is commercialization, that is, production of electrical generating equipment at home.

RESPONSES OF ALAN WM. WOLFF TO QUESTIONS FROM SENATOR CANTWELL

Question 1. As the top two energy consumers and greenhouse gas emitters in the world, I believe the United States and China have a tremendous opportunity to work together to solve their shared energy and environmental challenges. China is investing heavily in clean energy and that should be a huge market opportunity for the United States.

The scale of their growth can be mind-boggling. China attracted $45.4 billion worth of clean energy investments in 2011. And that's going to continue.

According to the International Energy Agency (IEA), to match its rapidly growing demand China needs to invest $3.7 trillion by 2030 to build over 1,300 Gigawatts of new electricity generating capacity. That's more than the total current installed capacity in the United States!

Clearly the U.S. has much to gain from cooperating with China on clean energy. Over the next decade, the Chinese government plans on spending $1 trillion to expand their railway network. The country will also build the equivalent of the United States' entire building stock in the next twenty-five years. Already in China today, some of the world's largest wind farms deliver power to cities over smart grid enabled, ultra-high-voltage long-distance transmission lines. China's vehicle mileage standards are higher than even our recently updated CAFE rules.

As the world's fastest- and largest-growing energy market, China is an ideal testing ground for scaling up and commercializing clean energy technologies. Combining our two energy markets increases economies of scale to bring down costs for consumers in both countries.

I see huge opportunities for U.S. technology exporters arising from a more cooperative relationship with China on clean energy because this is critical for our mutual efforts to produce clean abundant energy, mitigate climate change, and meet our long term emissions target. While we will certainly have to compete with each other, I think we need to follow what some call "co-opetition."

a. Do you agree that there is much more to gain for both the US and China from a cooperative framework on our mutual clean energy interests?

b. How would the witnesses characterize the extent of overlapping interests within the American and Chinese markets for clean energy?

Answer. I agree that there is much that can be gained from cooperation between China and the United States in increasing the production of clean energy and clean energy generating equipment. For this to occur, China would have to view cooperation rather than autarky as a path to greater use of renewable energy. There is no need for either country to go it alone. China would have to remove mercantilist "buy-Chinese" policies entirely and this would have to be reciprocated by the United States.

Question 2. Senator Murkowski and I sent a letter to President Obama with 13 other Senators urging him to strengthen cooperation with China on clean energy technology development and deployment. I was very pleased that Presidents Obama and Hu agreed on a clean energy package that included several measures to advance our relationship with China.

Many experts have recommended keeping pressure to open markets and to create an integrated US-China market for clean energy technologies. I introduced a Senate Resolution calling for the U.S. to work on eliminating tariff and non-tariff barriers to clean energy goods and services.

For the last several years, the United States and European Union have tried to eliminate tariffs and trade barriers to clean energy and environmental goods and services at the World Trade Organization (WTO). However, talks have stalled.

I think we need to try harder. Hundreds of billions of dollars in exports of clean energy and environmental goods and services are needed to get us to a clean energy future. But these tariffs and other trade issues are slowing us down and harming what could be a tremendous trade opportunity.

      a. Could eliminating tariffs and non-tariff barriers to trade in clean energy and environmental goods and services be beneficial to both countries?

      b. What particular mechanisms can we use to eliminate existing tariffs and non-tariff barriers on clean energy technologies?

Answer. I fully agree that it should be in both countries' interests for China to remove its trade barriers. These are not so much in the form of tariff and traditional nontariff barriers. The measures are not much at the border, they take the form of national policies implemented often through informal means by state-owned enterprises. Sometimes market barriers take the form of visible measures—standards, indigenous innovation mandates, procurement catalogs and the like. But there are hidden barriers due to the structure of the Chinese economy. For these, agreements have to concentrate on measurable results compared with markets as open as those of, for example, the European Union and the United States.

Question 3. Despite some of the recent news stories and trade complaints, all is not wrong with our clean energy relationship with China.

Emerging clean energy technologies are becoming increasingly competitive in the marketplace. For instance, solar power is now competitive with daytime retail power prices in a number of countries. Last month Bloomberg New Energy Finance released a report finding that average solar PV module prices have fallen by nearly 75 percent in the past three years. That same Bloomberg report found that these recent reductions in PV prices are likely to be sustainable, as they are primarily a reflection of reductions in manufacturing costs. Lowering the cost of clean energy, such as solar, is exactly what we need to be doing.

The affordability of solar energy has stimulated business investment and created jobs in most of the industry. Although much of the focus on solar energy has focused on one sector of the industry - manufacturing solar panels - it only accounts for roughly 5 percent of solar jobs in the United States. Over half of the jobs in the solar industry involve designing, installing, and maintaining solar energy systems.

I am concerned about the recent trade complaints and their effect on the over 2,000 solar employees in Washington state. Having the 12th largest solar workforce in the nation, mostly in other sectors of the solar industry, I think we need to be weary of the unintended consequences. Our trade actions could lead to retaliation on our own successful polysilicon industry, for example.

In my home state, REC Silicon has worked very hard to innovate and cut costs and has become the leading low-cost supplier of polysilicon in the world. Trade retaliation from China could endanger roughly 860 American manufacturing jobs that REC Silicon provides, and up to 49,589 jobs nationally.by 2014, according to a recent Brattle Group analysis.

My experience at a technology company taught me that innovation, scale, and American entrepreneurship will always figure out how to drive down costs over the long term. We will win with open markets, and that's why we need to continue pressing for open markets for clean energy rather than imposing new tariffs.

      a. Do you believe that the final result of these recent trade cases will be good for our clean energy industries as a whole?

      b. Do escalating trade complaints on all sides endanger growth, investments, and jobs in emerging clean energy industries?

Answer. While I support an industry's right to petition for and receive relief under the U.S. laws and consistent with U.S. rights and obligations under the WTO, whatever the result of the current case on solar, it does not constitute a national strategy for increasing the technological development, commercialization and deployment of solar energy in the United States. The country should not have a one-dimensional policy for solar energy, consisting solely of whether injury is found by an independent U.S. agency and dumping and subsidization are found by the Department of Commerce.

Question 4. While I am glad to see that the US led the world in private clean energy investment last year, this is just one inning of a long series. I am frankly concerned that we cannot sustain this leadership with the policies we have in place today - even if we extend all of the clean energy tax incentives later this year.

Pew recently profiled the national energy policies by country in its report "Who's Winning the Clean Energy Race." Of the eight key national clean energy policies listed in these country profiles, the US only has three in place - three of the eight - and those include clean energy tax incentives, which we still need to extend, and government procurement, which is increasingly under political attacks. China, in contrast, has six of the key eight national policies in place. And many of our European competitors (including Germany, France, the United Kingdom, and Italy) also have six or more of these critical policies.

This policy gap should be a call to action. We need to continue moving forward, not backward. We need to be working on more aggressive policies to seize this enormous global clean energy market opportunity rather than debating the ones we've already passed on a bipartisan basis.

While I have long advocated for bilateral clean energy cooperation with China, I also want to be sure that the United States is the world's leading supplier of clean energy technologies to meet the exploding world demand.

a. In terms of our international competitiveness going forward, what sort of incentives are in place in China to promote clean energy development and deployment and how do they compare to the U.S. from your perspective?

b. Do you believe that if we fail to create the right policies and investment incentives at home, we'll miss out on lucrative opportunities for global leadership in clean energy?

c. Wouldn't placing a clear price on carbon be one of the policies that would spur our clean energy industries?

Answer. There is something wrong with China's mix of policies when until very recently it produced a glut of solar cells and panels and only was able to absorb 5% or so at home (the figure has since been estimated to be during this year about 25%). The fact remains that China's record of deployment of solar and wind, and the degree to which these are grid-connected has not been good enough, and given China's economic growth, while it has been greatly increasing the deployment of renewable energy sources, the mix has in fact moved even more in the direction of using fossil fuels. I agree that we need to put into place the right mix of policies at home and maintain consistency in their application. Too many incentives are simply too uncertain in this country to call forth the private national effort needed to increase greatly the deployment of clean energies. In both countries, while hydro power is clean, it is also not feasible to greatly increase reliance on it, except to the extent that existing generating facilities can be made more efficient.

Question 5. Until the beginning of this Congress, there was an overwhelming consensus that clean energy incentives were a good thing. They worked and created jobs. Just a few years ago, the Cantwell-Ensign bill -- which extended many key clean energy credits and established the eight year ITC -- passed the Senate by a vote of 93 to 2.

There has been little success this Congress in reaching across the aisle to get these credits extended -- or to reform the existing credits to make them more effective. It has been an uphill battle, and certainly not for a lack of trying.

So what's changed? Why are credits which used to enjoy fairly broad support become so partisan? Many of those in Congress who have railed against our attempt to build this new industry have petitioned for clean energy projects for their constituents. And polling from Yale and George Mason University show that they oppose the majority of Americans who want to develop clean energy and invest in research.

So how do we get back on track? As many of you know we have already lost a lot of ground. Many important energy credits have already expired. Or in the case of wind, effectively expired given the placed-in-service requirement. In the short term, I believe that we must extend these credits to maintain the American clean energy jobs that they support.

a. Assuming comprehensive tax reform is not happening this year, will jobs be lost if we fail to extend these expiring credits that industries have been banking on?

b. On the flip side, will businesses create jobs if these provisions are extended for a predictable period of time?

c. As Congress begins to grapple with a major reform of the tax code, would you be willing to trade the certainty of multiyear extensions for a sunset date for all energy tax subsidies?

d. Do you think it's fair that some energy sources benefit from permanent subsidies and others have to deal with the uncertainty of short-term extensions?

Answer. If the mix of energy sources is to change toward renewables, they must benefit from greater economic incentives than traditional fossil fuels. These incentives can be in many forms—mandates, feed-in tariffs, direct government financial support and tax incentives. If there is a consensus that the national security and the country's environmental objectives require a change in the mix of energy sources, to point the way this must be reflected in the direct and indirect incentives offered.

Question 6. I want to ask about the scale of advanced energy R&D investment that we need. As you are surely well aware, the energy sector itself invests a far smaller fraction of its revenue in research and new technology development than many other sectors of the American economy. According to one analysis from the Breakthrough Institute, the energy sector invests just two tenths of one percent of annual revenues in R&D, an order of magnitude lower than the national average across all industries (2.6%) and two orders of magnitude lower than leading innovation-driven industries such as biotech, semiconductors or information technology.

The health care sector invests a full 20% of its revenues in R&D and the federal government adds to this with over $30 billion annually in health care research spending through the National Institutes of Health (NIH). Yet despite the far lower levels of private sector energy research spending, the federal government invests just a few billion annually in energy R&D, mostly through the Department of Energy (DOE).

With private sector investment levels like these, there seems to be a strong need for public investments that can fill the gap and help drive the innovation and advanced energy technologies we need. While we certainly have to make some difficult choices when it comes to getting our fiscal house in order, I do not believe critical investments in R&D are the path to a brighter fiscal and economic future. If securing our energy independence, averting climate change and creating new energy industries and jobs are true national priorities, shouldn't our energy R&D budgets be more on the scale of NIH?

Answer. You raise a key question. Just how high a priority is it for the United States to change the course of the country's energy policy to a much greater reliance on clean energy and particularly renewables? The United States in the context of WWII engaged in a herculean effort to master the forces of nuclear power, initially for weapons development but with enormous additional applications in peacetime, including nuclear fuel for power generation. A similar effort was incurred in the manned space flight program. I recognize that this is a time of budget stringency, but what if the cost of renewables could be driven down to the point where it made energy much less expensive. That investment would repay its costs hundreds if not thousands of times over in terms of a boost to U.S. competitiveness and jobs, not to mention national security through freeing the country from reliance on foreign offshore sources of energy. The value would be nearly incalculable. And this is without including the savings and beneficial health effects of reducing the pressures on the atmosphere leading to climate change. Is this a challenge on the order of magnitude and worthy of the investments to cure diseases? That case can and should be made.

Question 7. Biomass is one clean energy sector in which the United States is second to none. We account for roughly 23 percent of the world's installed capacity, compared to China's 7 percent share.

I do not believe this is a coincidence. The long-term market signal that the Renewable Fuel Standard (RFS) sends reduces the uncertainty and unleashes investment. This is precisely what is needed in other sectors - a long term signal that unleashes investment in clean energy.

I am proud that my state is at the forefront of figuring out alternative ways to produce jet fuel from a variety of non-petroleum domestic sources. A broad coalition of researchers, farmers, entrepreneurs, fuel producers, jet makers, airports, and others are all working together to figure out the best way to make green jet fuel. They believe that homegrown jet fuel alternatives will mean real economic growth in Washington state and can create jobs around the nation. They know that instead of sending billions overseas each year for foreign oil, we should be figuring out ways we can keep that money here at home, supporting our economy and workers.

The U.S. military is also leading the way on this opportunity. The U.S. Air Force is currently testing different blends of biofuels and jet fuels, and hopes to acquire 50 percent of its domestic aviation fuel from alternative fuel blends by 2016. The Air Force is the nation's largest user of energy, spending about $8 billion on fuel and electricity every year - about 84 percent of that goes to fuel our aircraft.

The U.S. Navy is also moving forward on biofuels. In an article in the Washington Post, Secretary of the Navy Ray Mabus said that, "[t]he main reason we're moving toward alternative fuels in the Navy and the Marine Corps is to make us better war fighters." Secretary Mabus went on to say that having a Marine either wounded or killed for every 50 convoys of fuel brought into Afghanistan is "just too high a price to pay."

a. Do you believe that the Department of Defense can play an important role in facilitating our emerging domestic biofuels industry?

b. Would these efforts advance our national security, both by decreasing our energy dependence and by reducing our military's expenditures on the full costs of energy over the long term?

Answer. DOD can certainly play an important role in the development of alternative forms of energy, including biofuels. In a broad sense, doing so will increase national security as it can decrease reliance on importing fuels from abroad, especially from sources that may prove unstable over time. If energy costs can be driven down, this will also serve to make defense budgets go further. However, in terms of support of troops deployed in remote locations, more important will be other forms of renewable energy such as solar, as well as improved conservation techniques (as relatively simple as improving insulation for portable living quarters). As long as a gallon of biofuels produces the same amount of energy as a gallon of traditional fuels, transporting the fuel over great distances to remote battlefields would not result in improved security.

RESPONSES OF DEREK SCISSORS TO QUESTIONS FROM SENATOR MURKOWSKI

ENERGY COSTS AS A FACTOR OF COMPETITIVENESS

Question 1. For all the talk of China's advances in clean energy manufacturing, the country is struggling mightily with environmental challenges. China has long since passed the United States in total greenhouse gas emissions and approximately one quarter of its water resources have been deemed unsafe. As I mentioned in my opening statement, the country's solar panel factories don't tend to run on solar power. The unfortunate irony of all this is that America has often relied upon the cheaper, dirtier manufacturing practices of China in order to affordably comply with requirements we've imposed on ourselves for cleaner, pricier energy here at home.

How significant is the role played by the cost and availability of energy in the United States' competitive position, compared to China's?

Answer. The American and Chinese approaches are very different. The U.S. has intervened less and most American intervention has been to discourage energy production for ecological reasons. Inhibiting coal production and oil transport raises the cost of energy, making American firms less competitive in energy-intensive activities, such as auto-making. Recent green energy subsidies promise competitiveness in a new field but rely in part on keeping traditional energy expensive, as well as diverting resources from elsewhere in the economy. The U.S. tends to hurt its competitiveness for the sake of the environment.

In contrast, the Chinese heavily subsidize energy consumption and it appears that energy very much helps their competitiveness. Among other things, subsidies have enabled electricity-intensive heavy industries such as steel to expand to huge proportions. The gain for China is more jobs in heavy industry and cheaper products, both for use at home and to sell overseas. China is more competitive in these areas than it would be with market prices for energy. However, in the PRC consumers subsidize producers, through anti-competitive regulation, the banking system, land acquisition bias, and so on. Ordinary people thus pay (even if they don't pay taxes) so heavy industry can expand. The other main cost is environmental. Both subsidizing heavy industry and making energy too cheap increases resource depletion and pollution.

The green energy push further reveals Chinese policy as wasteful. The PRC subsidizes coal consumption, making coal cheaper and increasing carbon emissions. It then must subsidize green energy more, to make it competitive with subsidized coal and to counter the emissions increase. For the last few years, Beijing has been fighting itself.

DEFINITION AND OUTSOURCING OF GREEN JOBS

Question 2. There was a bit of renewed interest in "green jobs" recently, when an administration witness testified that this category of employment includes everything from college professors and antique dealers to bicycle repair clerks and used record shop employees. In addition to these broad definitions, others have said that green jobs "can never be outsourced." Together, these claims have created a lot of confusion about—and, frankly, mistrust of—the pitches that have been made in support of stimulus spending and other activities.

How would each of you define the term "green job".or do you think we should even have a separate category for them—and do you think "green jobs" are any more or less susceptible to outsourcing than regular jobs?

Answer. The job classification issue is an old one. When American manufacturers in the 1960's began hiving off supporting activities such as accounting, human resources, etc. to specialized contractors, that came to be seen as lost jobs in manufacturing. But in many cases, the number of people involved in actual manufacturing did not change.

In green energy as in other sectors, the division should be (i) jobs in green energy, (ii) jobs green energy indirectly supports, and (iii) jobs that have less connection to green energy than other sectors and should not be counted (antique dealer, for example). Going beyond green energy jobs to "green jobs" is a mistake. If a green job is any job that is considered good for the environment, it will be impossible to compare green jobs to other kinds of jobs, because jobs measures are based on occupation, not impact.

For outsourcing, it is easier to outsource production than services. This is part of the reason our service sector is larger than our manufacturing sector. If green jobs are thought to be concentrated in services, they would be harder to outsource than jobs in general. Green services jobs can still be outsourced, though. For example, an environmental consulting firm that advises companies on how to reduce their carbon footprint can be located anywhere.

Green jobs involving energy production are just as easy to outsource as other energy production jobs. Electricity generation tends to stay close to home but the materials needed to create electricity, from crude oil to wind turbines, can be outsourced no matter whether they are green or not.

RESPONSES OF DEREK SCISSORS TO QUESTIONS FROM SENATOR CANTWELL

Question 1. As the top two energy consumers and greenhouse gas emitters in the world, I believe the United States and China have a tremendous opportunity to work together to solve their shared energy and environmental challenges. China is investing heavily in clean energy and that should be a huge market opportunity for the United States.

The scale of their growth can be mind-boggling. China attracted $45.4 billion worth of clean energy investments in 2011. And that's going to continue. According to the International Energy Agency (IEA), to match its rapidly growing demand China needs to invest $3.7 trillion by 2030 to build over 1,300 Gigawatts of new electricity generating capacity. That's more than the total current installed capacity in the United States!

Clearly the U.S. has much to gain from cooperating with China on clean energy. Over the next decade, the Chinese government plans on spending $1 trillion to expand their railway network. The country will also build the equivalent of the United States' entire building stock in the next twenty-five years. Already in China today, some of the world's largest wind farms deliver power to cities over smart grid enabled, ultra-high-voltage long-distance transmission lines. China's vehicle mileage standards are higher than even our recently updated CAFE rules.

As the world's fastest-and largest-growing energy market, China is an ideal testing ground for scaling up and commercializing clean energy technologies. Combining our two energy markets increases economies of scale to bring down costs for consumers in both countries.

I see huge opportunities for U.S. technology exporters arising from a more cooperative relationship with China on clean energy because this is critical for our mutual efforts to produce clean abundant energy, mitigate climate change, and meet our long term emissions target. While we will certainly have to compete with each other, I think we need to follow what some call "co-opetition."

    a. Do you agree that there is much more to gain for both the US and China from a cooperative framework on our mutual clean energy interests?

    b. How would the witnesses characterize the extent of overlapping interests within the American and Chinese markets for clean energy?

Answer. There is potential for valuable and very extensive cooperation in clean energy between the U.S. and PRC, the world's two largest economies, two largest energy producers, and two largest clean energy investors. This cooperation can range from simple energy trade that changes China's energy mix to two-way investment to joint research. These avenues should be explored.

Expectations should be limited, though, due to the lack of overlapping interests. The PRC has explicitly required state control of its energy sector. Energy is obviously crucial to the industrial expansion that has created enough jobs to keep the Communist Party in power during a period where the labor force has greatly expanded (for an example of what happens when the labor force expands and job creation is insufficient, see the Arab world.) There is no sign at present that Beijing is willing to relax state control of the energy industry.

American goals of innovation, energy efficiency, and limiting carbon emissions are secondary for China to state control, low cost, and job creation. This is evident in the PRC's simultaneous subsidies for coal consumption and green energy production for export (chiefly solar panels and wind turbines). Both countries value self-sufficiency but, of course, that does not favor more trade and investment. While the U.S. will look first for technological breakthroughs for the sake of energy efficiency, low emissions, and self-sufficiency, China looks first at turning technology into jobs via state regulatory and financial actions, including actions that take jobs away from their trade partners.

Cooperation should be pursued to the extent Beijing allows it. But, as in so many other sectors, the promise of the Chinese market is unlikely to be realized unless there are very considerable policy changes.

Question 2. Senator Murkowski and I sent a letter to President Obama with 13 other Senators urging him to strengthen cooperation with China on clean energy technology development and deployment. I was very pleased that Presidents Obama and Hu agreed on a clean energy package that included several measures to advance our relationship with China.

Many experts have recommended keeping pressure to open markets and to create an integrated US-China market for clean energy technologies. I introduced a Senate Resolution calling for the U.S. to work on eliminating tariff and non-tariff barriers to clean energy goods and services.

For the last several years, the United States and European Union have tried to eliminate tariffs and trade barriers to clean energy and environmental goods and services at the World Trade Organization (WTO). However, talks have stalled.

I think we need to try harder. Hundreds of billions of dollars in exports of clean energy and environmental goods and services are needed to get us to a clean energy future. But these tariffs and other trade issues are slowing us down and harming what could be a tremendous trade opportunity.

> a. Could eliminating tariffs and non-tariff barriers to trade in clean energy and environmental goods and services be beneficial to both countries?
> b. What particular mechanisms can we use to eliminate existing tariffs and non-tariff barriers on clean energy technologies?

Answer. A global agreement to reduce tariff and non-tariff barriers in environmental trade would be a major breakthrough and is worth a great deal of effort.

Some countries will seek to substitute non-tariff barriers for tariffs. It is thus useful to start with countries truly committed to open environmental trade. With the WTO stalled, the U.S. and EU should proceed on their own, dropping all barriers to environmental goods and services between the two. There should be a standing invitation to all other countries to observe and, if they meet conditions on non-tariff barriers, to join the group. The Information Technology Agreement is an obvious model and could conceivably be extended for those ITA parties which make sufficient commitments on non-tariff barriers.

A global agreement would be ideal but is not currently possible. A multilateral agreement would be quite helpful and also exert pressure toward a global agreement.

Question 3. Despite some of the recent news stories and trade complaints, all is not wrong with our clean energy relationship with China.

Emerging clean energy technologies are becoming increasingly competitive in the marketplace. For instance, solar power is now competitive with daytime retail power prices in a number of countries. Last month Bloomberg New Energy Finance released a report finding that average solar PV module prices have fallen by nearly 75 percent in the past three years. That same Bloomberg report found that these recent reductions in PV prices are likely to be sustainable, as they are primarily a reflection of reductions in manufacturing costs. Lowering the cost of clean energy, such as solar, is exactly what we need to be doing.

The affordability of solar energy has stimulated business investment and created jobs in most of the industry. Although much of the focus on solar energy has focused on one sector of the industry—manufacturing solar panels—it only accounts for roughly 5 percent of solar jobs in the United States. Over half of the jobs in the solar industry involve designing, installing, and maintaining solar energy systems.

I am concerned about the recent trade complaints and their effect on the over 2,000 solar employees in Washington state. Having the 12th largest solar workforce in the nation, mostly in other sectors of the solar industry, I think we need to be weary of the unintended consequences. Our trade actions could lead to retaliation on our own successful polysilicon industry, for example.

In my home state, REC Silicon has worked very hard to innovate and cut costs and has become the leading low-cost supplier of polysilicon in the world. Trade retaliation from China could endanger roughly 860 American manufacturing jobs that REC Silicon provides, and up to 49,589 jobs nationally.by 2014, according to a recent Brattle Group analysis.

My experience at a technology company taught me that innovation, scale, and American entrepreneurship will always figure out how to drive down costs over the long term. We will win with open markets, and that's why we need to continue pressing for open markets for clean energy rather than imposing new tariffs.

a. Do you believe that the final result of these recent trade cases will be good for our clean energy industries as a whole?

b. Do escalating trade complaints on all sides endanger growth, investments, and jobs in emerging clean energy industries?

Answer. The environmental trade complaints against China are understandable in an important respect: China heavily subsidizes its environmental exports and these subsidies distort world trade. As a pure trade correction, the complaints have merit.

With regard to our energy and environmental goals, however, the trade cases are harmful. The original point of the clean energy industry was to reduce carbon emissions and achieve other ecological goals. Competition from imports can only bring these goals closer, while blocking this competition will raise the price of clean energy and discourage its use. If the primary goal is now job creation, jobs can much more easily be created in coal and gas than in solar and wind. The trade cases depart from the clean energy industry's reason for being.

Global trade and investment tensions in clean energy threaten ecological goals by raising costs and inhibiting innovation, both of which flow from competition. Behind these trade complaints is the view that clean energy is primarily about jobs, rather than limiting emissions, for example. On this view, clean energy should be just another target for industrial policy, inviting government intervention and seeing foreign companies as harmful. An industrial policy approach to clean energy will stifle innovation, efficiency, and growth, making the enterprise much more expensive and wasteful than necessary.

Question 4. While I am glad to see that the US led the world in private clean energy investment last year, this is just one inning of a long series. I am frankly concerned that we cannot sustain this leadership with the policies we have in place today—even if we extend all of the clean energy tax incentives later this year.

Pew recently profiled the national energy policies by country in its report "Who's Winning the Clean Energy Race." Of the eight key national clean energy policies listed in these country profiles, the US only has three in place—three of the eight—and those include clean energy tax incentives, which we still need to extend, and government procurement, which is increasingly under political attacks. China, in contrast, has six of the key eight national policies in place. And many of our European competitors (including Germany, France, the United Kingdom, and Italy) also have six or more of these critical policies.

This policy gap should be a call to action. We need to continue moving forward, not backward. We need to be working on more aggressive policies to seize this enormous global clean energy market opportunity rather than debating the ones we've already passed on a bipartisan basis.

While I have long advocated for bilateral clean energy cooperation with China, I also want to be sure that the United States is the world's leading supplier of clean energy technologies to meet the exploding world demand.

a. In terms of our international competitiveness going forward, what sort of incentives are in place in China to promote clean energy development and deployment and how do they compare to the U.S. from your perspective?

b. Do you believe that if we fail to create the right policies and investment incentives at home, we'll miss out on lucrative opportunities for global leadership in clean energy?

c. Wouldn't placing a clear price on carbon be one of the policies that would spur our clean energy industries?

Answer. Chinese energy policies as a whole are an abysmal failure. The reliance on coal has been increasing (after falling in the late 1990's), the first large-scale coal imports have begun, energy self-sufficiency as a whole has declined, energy efficiency has improved more slowly than necessary, carbon emissions have soared, and many Chinese clean energy companies are sliding into deep debt. All China has to offer in clean energy is policy and regulatory language that has to this point proven largely empty and huge amounts of spending, most of which serves to remedy the ills of its broader energy policies. This is not a model for the U.S.

There is a trade-off between global commercial leadership in clean energy and the environmental goals that brought the industry into being. The U.S. can choose policies to make American companies artificially competitive in clean energy, at the cost of provoking our global partners. But this merely shifts the cost of clean energy onto the taxpayer, it does not truly make clean energy more efficient. Alternately, the U.S. can set ecological goals and take no stance on which countries and firms lead in clean energy. Failing to make a choice will lead to policy that bounces back and forth between objectives, as in the solar trade cases, and risks accomplishing very little.

Carbon is already clearly priced. The market failure is that the price on carbon does not fully reflect its environmental impact and thus is too low. Directly setting an artificial price for carbon would be very harmful—price controls warp markets in often surprising and always damaging ways. A carbon tax, on top of a flexible market price, is superior to setting a price outright. The amount and timing of a tax are major issues but an initially low tax as part of broader, pro-growth tax reform would serve as an experiment to see how clean energy development would respond.

Question 5. Until the beginning of this Congress, there was an overwhelming consensus that clean energy incentives were a good thing. They worked and created jobs. Just a few years ago, the Cantwell-Ensign bill—which extended many key clean energy credits and established the eight year ITC—passed the Senate by a vote of 93 to 2.

There has been little success this Congress in reaching across the aisle to get these credits extended—or to reform the existing credits to make them more effective. It has been an uphill battle, and certainly not for a lack of trying.

So what's changed? Why are credits which used to enjoy fairly broad support become so partisan? Many of those in Congress who have railed against our attempt to build this new industry have petitioned for clean energy projects for their constituents. And polling from Yale and George Mason University show that they oppose the majority of Americans who want to develop clean energy and invest in research.

So how do we get back on track? As you know we have already lost a lot of ground. Many important energy credits have already expired. Or in the case of wind, effectively expired given the placed-in-service requirement. In the short term, I believe that we must extend these credits to maintain the American clean energy jobs that they support.

   a. Assuming comprehensive tax reform is not happening this year, will jobs be lost if we fail to extend these expiring credits that industries have been banking on?

   b. On the flip side, will businesses create jobs if these provisions are extended for a predictable period of time?

   c. As Congress begins to grapple with a major reform of the tax code, would you be willing to trade the certainty of multiyear extensions for a sunset date for all energy tax subsidies?

   d. Do you think it's fair that some energy sources benefit from permanent subsidies and others have to deal with the uncertainty of short-term extensions?

Answer. The net effect on jobs of letting credits expire or extending them cannot be calculated without specifying what the resources would otherwise be used for. In a truly awful fiscal setting, just creating jobs is not enough. An exceptional number of jobs must be created. It is true that consistency and clarity in the regulatory environment will improve the outcome regardless of whether extension or expiration is chosen.

There are huge gains possible in tax reform. One such gain would be ending all energy subsidies as quickly as possible. That would be far, far better than dueling government subsidies for competing types of energy production, where the government is effectively paying all sides. This is the worst possible outcome. No sector should benefit from any sort of subsidy, much less a permanent one.

Question 6. I want to ask about the scale of advanced energy R&D investment that we need. As you are surely well aware, the energy sector itself invests a far smaller fraction of its revenue in research and new technology development than many other sectors of the American economy. According to one analysis from the Breakthrough Institute, the energy sector invests just two tenths of one percent of annual revenues in R&D, an order of magnitude lower than the national average across all industries (2.6%) and two orders of magnitude lower than leading innovation-driven industries such as biotech, semiconductors or information technology.

The health care sector invests a full 20% of its revenues in R&D and the federal government adds to this with over $30 billion annually in health care research spending through the National Institutes of Health (NIH). Yet despite the far lower levels of private sector energy research spending, the federal government invests just a few billion annually in energy R&D, mostly through the Department of Energy (DOE).

With private sector investment levels like these, there seems to be a strong need for public investments that can fill the gap and help drive the innovation and advanced energy technologies we need. While we certainly have to make some difficult choices when it comes to getting our fiscal house in order, I do not believe critical investments in R&D are the path to a brighter fiscal and economic future. If securing our energy independence, averting climate change and creating new energy industries and jobs are true national priorities, shouldn't our energy R&D budgets be more on the scale of NIH?

Answer. One reason the revenue share of energy investment appears low is that exploration is often not counted as research.

Putting that aside, there is an important role for government in basic research. There is little point in starting a basic research program only for the short-term, though, so government-sponsored research must be fiscally sustainable. Once a sustainable fiscal course is set, the government must resist the urge to support applied research. When the government starts to influence the commercial path, the result is inevitably harmful because the government is not a commercial entity. If public R&D is both fiscally sustainable and purely basic research, a large budget would be helpful in energy.

Question 7. Biomass is one clean energy sector in which the United States is second to none. We account for roughly 23 percent of the world's installed capacity, compared to China's 7 percent share.

I do not believe this is a coincidence. The long-term market signal that the Renewable Fuel Standard (RFS) sends reduces the uncertainty and unleashes investment. This is precisely what is needed in other sectors—a long term signal that unleashes investment in clean energy.

I am proud that my state is at the forefront of figuring out alternative ways to produce jet fuel from a variety of non-petroleum domestic sources. A broad coalition of researchers, farmers, entrepreneurs, fuel producers, jet makers, airports, and others are all working together to figure out the best way to make green jet fuel. They believe that homegrown jet fuel alternatives will mean real economic growth in Washington state and can create jobs around the nation. They know that instead of sending billions overseas each year for foreign oil, we should be figuring out ways we can keep that money here at home, supporting our economy and workers.

The U.S. military is also leading the way on this opportunity. The U.S. Air Force is currently testing different blends of biofuels and jet fuels, and hopes to acquire 50 percent of its domestic aviation fuel from alternative fuel blends by 2016. The Air Force is the nation's largest user of energy, spending about $8 billion on fuel and electricity every year—about 84 percent of that goes to fuel our aircraft.

The U.S. Navy is also moving forward on biofuels. In an article in the Washington Post, Secretary of the Navy Ray Mabus said that, "[t]he main reason we're moving toward alternative fuels in the Navy and the Marine Corps is to make us better war fighters." Secretary Mabus went on to say that having a Marine either wounded or killed for every 50 convoys of fuel brought into Afghanistan is "just too high a price to pay."

   a. Do you believe that the Department of Defense can play an important role in facilitating our emerging domestic biofuels industry?
   b. Would these efforts advance our national security, both by decreasing our energy dependence and by reducing our military's expenditures on the full costs of energy over the long term?

Answer. The Department of Defense can play an important role in encouraging biofuels but it might be damaging if it does. DOD must focus exclusively on its primary mission; detours into energy policy are an awful idea.

If DOD finds that changing its fuel mix, for example, enhances the primary mission, it will certainly affect the domestic energy market because DOD is such a large player. But the effect may not be for the better. DOD's fuel needs do not reflect the needs of typical energy users and may (or may not) skew prices and supply in a way that harms other market participants. Again, this should not enter DOD's own calculus, either way.

The broad national security evaluation cannot be made solely by DOD, it requires inter-agency coordination. Decisions concerning energy dependence are of sufficient importance that such coordination should involve the President. It should be noted that American dependence on foreign energy is currently decreasing.

Question 8. Dr. Scissors, I noticed in your testimony that you believe a primary reason for China's aggressive action on clean energy is to create jobs and that renewables support more jobs compared to fossil fuels. Could you please elaborate on this further?

I understand and support our desire to become a more efficient nation, and this committee has worked on just that over the years. But it's still not clear to me why you think we should give up and stop competing with China for clean energy jobs. We need jobs—today and in the future. Considering that clean energy may be one of the largest market opportunities of the 21st century, where will find enough jobs if we stop competing for jobs in one of the largest emerging markets?

Answer. The history of the Chinese clean energy industry starts with a response to clean energy subsidies in Europe, not any ecological goals in China itself. The vast majority of solar products have been exported, creating jobs but not improving the environment. Chinese performance on emissions, energy efficiency, and self-sufficiency has been terrible, indicating these are not the main objectives. At this stage in their development, renewables require more labor to generate the same amount of electricity as fossil fuels. If the goal is job creation, as in China, renewables therefore seem attractive. If the goal is energy efficiency, renewable are less efficient and less attractive.

There are two main reasons not to focus on jobs. First, making jobs the goal also heightens trade conflicts, because jobs are unavoidably seen as zero-sum to a certain extent. Making efficiency the goal encourages open trade,.

Second and more fundamental, emphasizing jobs puts the cart before the horse. Clean energy is considered to be a leading market opportunity because it could bring enormous environmental benefits. Promoting those benefits argue for making clean energy as cost-effective and efficient as possible. Targeting jobs is a quite different matter—it raises costs and reduces efficiency. In my view, an emphasis on jobs warps the reason the clean energy industry is valuable in the first place.

[Responses to the following questions were not received at the time the hearing went to press:]

QUESTIONS FOR CLYDE PRESTOWITZ FROM SENATOR MURKOWSKI

ENERGY COSTS AS A FACTOR OF COMPETITIVENESS

Question 1. For all the talk of China's advances in clean energy manufacturing, the country is struggling mightily with environmental challenges. China has long since passed the United States in total greenhouse gas emissions and approximately one quarter of its water resources have been deemed unsafe. As I mentioned in my opening statement, the country's solar panel factories don't tend to run on solar power. The unfortunate irony of all this is that America has often relied upon the cheaper, dirtier manufacturing practices of China in order to affordably comply with requirements we've imposed on ourselves for cleaner, pricier energy here at home.

  a. How significant is the role played by the cost and availability of energy in the United States' competitive position, compared to China's?

DEFINITION AND OUTSOURCING OF GREEN JOBS

Question 2. There was a bit of renewed interest in "green jobs" recently, when an administration witness testified that this category of employment includes everything from college professors and antique dealers to bicycle repair clerks and used record shop employees. In addition to these broad definitions, others have said that green jobs "can never be outsourced." Together, these claims have created a lot of confusion about—and, frankly, mistrust of—the pitches that have been made in support of stimulus spending and other activities.

  a. How would each of you define the term "green job"—or do you think we should even have a separate category for them—and do you think "green jobs" are any more or less susceptible to outsourcing than regular jobs?

QUESTIONS FOR CLYDE PRESTOWITZ FROM SENATOR CANTWELL

Question 1. As the top two energy consumers and greenhouse gas emitters in the world, I believe the United States and China have a tremendous opportunity to work together to solve their shared energy and environmental challenges. China is investing heavily in clean energy and that should be a huge market opportunity for the United States.

The scale of their growth can be mind-boggling. China attracted $45.4 billion worth of clean energy investments in 2011. And that's going to continue. According to the International Energy Agency (IEA), to match its rapidly growing demand China needs to invest $3.7 trillion by 2030 to build over 1,300 Gigawatts of new electricity generating capacity. That's more than the total current installed capacity in the United States!

Clearly the U.S. has much to gain from cooperating with China on clean energy. Over the next decade, the Chinese government plans on spending $1 trillion to expand their railway network. The country will also build the equivalent of the United States' entire building stock in the next twenty-five years. Already in China today, some of the world's largest wind farms deliver power to cities over smart grid enabled, ultra-high-voltage long-distance transmission lines. China's vehicle mileage standards are higher than even our recently updated CAFE rules.

As the world's fastest-and largest-growing energy market, China is an ideal testing ground for scaling up and commercializing clean energy technologies. Combining our two energy markets increases economies of scale to bring down costs for consumers in both countries.

I see huge opportunities for U.S. technology exporters arising from a more cooperative relationship with China on clean energy because this is critical for our mutual efforts to produce clean abundant energy, mitigate climate change, and meet our long term emissions target. While we will certainly have to compete with each other, I think we need to follow what some call "co-opetition."

 a. Do you agree that there is much more to gain for both the US and China from a cooperative framework on our mutual clean energy interests?
 b. How would the witnesses characterize the extent of overlapping interests within the American and Chinese markets for clean energy?

Question 2. Senator Murkowski and I sent a letter to President Obama with 13 other Senators urging him to strengthen cooperation with China on clean energy technology development and deployment. I was very pleased that Presidents Obama and Hu agreed on a clean energy package that included several measures to advance our relationship with China.

Many experts have recommended keeping pressure to open markets and to create an integrated US-China market for clean energy technologies. I introduced a Senate Resolution calling for the U.S. to work on eliminating tariff and non-tariff barriers to clean energy goods and services.

For the last several years, the United States and European Union have tried to eliminate tariffs and trade barriers to clean energy and environmental goods and services at the World Trade Organization (WTO). However, talks have stalled.

I think we need to try harder. Hundreds of billions of dollars in exports of clean energy and environmental goods and services are needed to get us to a clean energy future. But these tariffs and other trade issues are slowing us down and harming what could be a tremendous trade opportunity.

 a. Could eliminating tariffs and non-tariff barriers to trade in clean energy and environmental goods and services be beneficial to both countries?
 b. What particular mechanisms can we use to eliminate existing tariffs and non-tariff barriers on clean energy technologies?

Question 3. Despite some of the recent news stories and trade complaints, all is not wrong with our clean energy relationship with China.

Emerging clean energy technologies are becoming increasingly competitive in the marketplace. For instance, solar power is now competitive with daytime retail power prices in a number of countries. Last month Bloomberg New Energy Finance released a report finding that average solar PV module prices have fallen by nearly 75 percent in the past three years. That same Bloomberg report found that these recent reductions in PV prices are likely to be sustainable, as they are primarily a reflection of reductions in manufacturing costs. Lowering the cost of clean energy, such as solar, is exactly what we need to be doing.

The affordability of solar energy has stimulated business investment and created jobs in most of the industry. Although much of the focus on solar energy has focused on one sector of the industry—manufacturing solar panels—it only accounts for roughly 5 percent of solar jobs in the United States. Over half of the jobs in the solar industry involve designing, installing, and maintaining solar energy systems.

I am concerned about the recent trade complaints and their effect on the over 2,000 solar employees in Washington state. Having the 12th largest solar workforce in the nation, mostly in other sectors of the solar industry, I think we need to be weary of the unintended consequences. Our trade actions could lead to retaliation on our own successful polysilicon industry, for example.

In my home state, REC Silicon has worked very hard to innovate and cut costs and has become the leading low-cost supplier of polysilicon in the world. Trade retaliation from China could endanger roughly 860 American manufacturing jobs that REC Silicon provides, and up to 49,589 jobs nationally.by 2014, according to a recent Brattle Group analysis.

My experience at a technology company taught me that innovation, scale, and American entrepreneurship will always figure out how to drive down costs over the long term. We will win with open markets, and that's why we need to continue pressing for open markets for clean energy rather than imposing new tariffs.

> a. Do you believe that the final result of these recent trade cases will be good for our clean energy industries as a whole?
> b. Do escalating trade complaints on all sides endanger growth, investments, and jobs in emerging clean energy industries?

Question 4. While I am glad to see that the US led the world in private clean energy investment last year, this is just one inning of a long series. I am frankly concerned that we cannot sustain this leadership with the policies we have in place today—even if we extend all of the clean energy tax incentives later this year.

Pew recently profiled the national energy policies by country in its report "Who's Winning the Clean Energy Race." Of the eight key national clean energy policies listed in these country profiles, the US only has three in place—three of the eight—and those include clean energy tax incentives, which we still need to extend, and government procurement, which is increasingly under political attacks. China, in contrast, has six of the key eight national policies in place. And many of our European competitors (including Germany, France, the United Kingdom, and Italy) also have six or more of these critical policies.

This policy gap should be a call to action. We need to continue moving forward, not backward. We need to be working on more aggressive policies to seize this enormous global clean energy market opportunity rather than debating the ones we've already passed on a bipartisan basis.

While I have long advocated for bilateral clean energy cooperation with China, I also want to be sure that the United States is the world's leading supplier of clean energy technologies to meet the exploding world demand.

> a. In terms of our international competitiveness going forward, what sort of incentives are in place in China to promote clean energy development and deployment and how do they compare to the U.S. from your perspective?
> b. Do you believe that if we fail to create the right policies and investment incentives at home, we'll miss out on lucrative opportunities for global leadership in clean energy?
> c. Wouldn't placing a clear price on carbon be one of the policies that would spur our clean energy industries?

Question 5. Until the beginning of this Congress, there was an overwhelming consensus that clean energy incentives were a good thing. They worked and created jobs. Just a few years ago, the Cantwell-Ensign bill—which extended many key clean energy credits and established the eight year ITC—passed the Senate by a vote of 93 to 2.

There has been little success this Congress in reaching across the aisle to get these credits extended—or to reform the existing credits to make them more effective. It has been an uphill battle, and certainly not for a lack of trying.

So what's changed? Why are credits which used to enjoy fairly broad support become so partisan? Many of those in Congress who have railed against our attempt to build this new industry have petitioned for clean energy projects for their constituents. And polling from Yale and George Mason University show that they oppose the majority of Americans who want to develop clean energy and invest in research.

So how do we get back on track? As many of you know we have already lost a lot of ground. Many important energy credits have already expired. Or in the case of wind, effectively expired given the placed-in-service requirement. In the short term, I believe that we must extend these credits to maintain the American clean energy jobs that they support.

> a. Assuming comprehensive tax reform is not happening this year, will jobs be lost if we fail to extend these expiring credits that industries have been banking on?

b. On the flip side, will businesses create jobs if these provisions are extended for a predictable period of time?

a. As Congress begins to grapple with a major reform of the tax code, would

c. you be willing to trade the certainty of multiyear extensions for a sunset date for all energy tax subsidies?

d. Do you think it's fair that some energy sources benefit from permanent subsidies and others have to deal with the uncertainty of short-term extensions?

Question 6. I want to ask about the scale of advanced energy R&D investment that we need. As you are surely well aware, the energy sector itself invests a far smaller fraction of its revenue in research and new technology development than many other sectors of the American economy. According to one analysis from the Breakthrough Institute, the energy sector invests just two tenths of one percent of annual revenues in R&D, an order of magnitude lower than the national average across all industries (2.6%) and two orders of magnitude lower than leading innovation-driven industries such as biotech, semiconductors or information technology.

The health care sector invests a full 20% of its revenues in R&D and the federal government adds to this with over $30 billion annually in health care research spending through the National Institutes of Health (NIH). Yet despite the far lower levels of private sector energy research spending, the federal government invests just a few billion annually in energy R&D, mostly through the Department of Energy (DOE).

With private sector investment levels like these, there seems to be a strong need for public investments that can fill the gap and help drive the innovation and advanced energy technologies we need. While we certainly have to make some difficult choices when it comes to getting our fiscal house in order, I do not believe critical investments in R&D are the path to a brighter fiscal and economic future. If securing our energy independence, averting climate change and creating new energy industries and jobs are true national priorities, shouldn't our energy R&D budgets be more on the scale of NIH?

Question 7. Biomass is one clean energy sector in which the United States is second to none. We account for roughly 23 percent of the world's installed capacity, compared to China's 7 percent share.

I do not believe this is a coincidence. The long-term market signal that the Renewable Fuel Standard (RFS) sends reduces the uncertainty and unleashes investment. This is precisely what is needed in other sectors—a long term signal that unleashes investment in clean energy.

I am proud that my state is at the forefront of figuring out alternative ways to produce jet fuel from a variety of non-petroleum domestic sources. A broad coalition of researchers, farmers, entrepreneurs, fuel producers, jet makers, airports, and others are all working together to figure out the best way to make green jet fuel. They believe that homegrown jet fuel alternatives will mean real economic growth in Washington state and can create jobs around the nation. They know that instead of sending billions overseas each year for foreign oil, we should be figuring out ways we can keep that money here at home, supporting our economy and workers.

The U.S. military is also leading the way on this opportunity. The U.S. Air Force is currently testing different blends of biofuels and jet fuels, and hopes to acquire 50 percent of its domestic aviation fuel from alternative fuel blends by 2016. The Air Force is the nation's largest user of energy, spending about $8 billion on fuel and electricity every year—about 84 percent of that goes to fuel our aircraft.

The U.S. Navy is also moving forward on biofuels. In an article in the Washington Post, Secretary of the Navy Ray Mabus said that, "[t]he main reason we're moving toward alternative fuels in the Navy and the Marine Corps is to make us better war fighters." Secretary Mabus went on to say that having a Marine either wounded or killed for every 50 convoys of fuel brought into Afghanistan is "just too high a price to pay."

a. Do you believe that the Department of Defense can play an important role in facilitating our emerging domestic biofuels industry?

b. Would these efforts advance our national security, both by decreasing our energy dependence and by reducing our military's expenditures on the full costs of energy over the long term?

QUESTIONS FOR JUSTIN WU FROM SENATOR MURKOWSKI

ENERGY COSTS AS A FACTOR OF COMPETITIVENESS

Question 1. For all the talk of China's advances in clean energy manufacturing, the country is struggling mightily with environmental challenges. China has long since passed the United States in total greenhouse gas emissions and approximately one quarter of its water resources have been deemed unsafe. As I mentioned in my opening statement, the country's solar panel factories don't tend to run on solar power. The unfortunate irony of all this is that America has often relied upon the cheaper, dirtier manufacturing practices of China in order to affordably comply with requirements we've imposed on ourselves for cleaner, pricier energy here at home.

a. How significant is the role played by the cost and availability of energy in the United States' competitive position, compared to China's?

DEFINITION AND OUTSOURCING OF GREEN JOBS

Question 2. There was a bit of renewed interest in "green jobs" recently, when an administration witness testified that this category of employment includes everything from college professors and antique dealers to bicycle repair clerks and used record shop employees. In addition to these broad definitions, others have said that green jobs "can never be outsourced." Together, these claims have created a lot of confusion about—and, frankly, mistrust of—the pitches that have been made in support of stimulus spending and other activities.

a. How would each of you define the term "green job"—or do you think we should even have a separate category for them—and do you think "green jobs" are any more or less susceptible to outsourcing than regular jobs?

QUESTIONS FOR JUSTIN WU FROM SENATOR CANTWELL

Question 1. As the top two energy consumers and greenhouse gas emitters in the world, I believe the United States and China have a tremendous opportunity to work together to solve their shared energy and environmental challenges. China is investing heavily in clean energy and that should be a huge market opportunity for the United States.

The scale of their growth can be mind-boggling. China attracted $45.4 billion worth of clean energy investments in 2011. And that's going to continue. According to the International Energy Agency (IEA), to match its rapidly growing demand China needs to invest $3.7 trillion by 2030 to build over 1,300 Gigawatts of new electricity generating capacity. That's more than the total current installed capacity in the United States!

Clearly the U.S. has much to gain from cooperating with China on clean energy. Over the next decade, the Chinese government plans on spending $1 trillion to expand their railway network. The country will also build the equivalent of the United States' entire building stock in the next twenty-five years. Already in China today, some of the world's largest wind farms deliver power to cities over smart grid enabled, ultra-high-voltage long-distance transmission lines. China's vehicle mileage standards are higher than even our recently updated CAFE rules.

As the world's fastest-and largest-growing energy market, China is an ideal testing ground for scaling up and commercializing clean energy technologies. Combining our two energy markets increases economies of scale to bring down costs for consumers in both countries.

I see huge opportunities for U.S. technology exporters arising from a more cooperative relationship with China on clean energy because this is critical for our mutual efforts to produce clean abundant energy, mitigate climate change, and meet our long term emissions target. While we will certainly have to compete with each other, I think we need to follow what some call "co-opetition."

a. Do you agree that there is much more to gain for both the US and China from a cooperative framework on our mutual clean energy interests?

b. How would the witnesses characterize the extent of overlapping interests within the American and Chinese markets for clean energy?

Question 2. Senator Murkowski and I sent a letter to President Obama with 13 other Senators urging him to strengthen cooperation with China on clean energy technology development and deployment. I was very pleased that Presidents Obama and Hu agreed on a clean energy package that included several measures to advance our relationship with China.

Many experts have recommended keeping pressure to open markets and to create an integrated US-China market for clean energy technologies. I introduced a Senate Resolution calling for the U.S. to work on eliminating tariff and non-tariff barriers to clean energy goods and services.

For the last several years, the United States and European Union have tried to eliminate tariffs and trade barriers to clean energy and environmental goods and services at the World Trade Organization (WTO). However, talks have stalled.

I think we need to try harder. Hundreds of billions of dollars in exports of clean energy and environmental goods and services are needed to get us to a clean energy future. But these tariffs and other trade issues are slowing us down and harming what could be a tremendous trade opportunity.

    a. Could eliminating tariffs and non-tariff barriers to trade in clean energy and environmental goods and services be beneficial to both countries?

    b. What particular mechanisms can we use to eliminate existing tariffs and non-tariff barriers on clean energy technologies?

Question 3. Despite some of the recent news stories and trade complaints, all is not wrong with our clean energy relationship with China.

Emerging clean energy technologies are becoming increasingly competitive in the marketplace. For instance, solar power is now competitive with daytime retail power prices in a number of countries. Last month Bloomberg New Energy Finance released a report finding that average solar PV module prices have fallen by nearly 75 percent in the past three years. That same Bloomberg report found that these recent reductions in PV prices are likely to be sustainable, as they are primarily a reflection of reductions in manufacturing costs. Lowering the cost of clean energy, such as solar, is exactly what we need to be doing.

The affordability of solar energy has stimulated business investment and created jobs in most of the industry. Although much of the focus on solar energy has focused on one sector of the industry—manufacturing solar panels—it only accounts for roughly 5 percent of solar jobs in the United States. Over half of the jobs in the solar industry involve designing, installing, and maintaining solar energy systems.

I am concerned about the recent trade complaints and their effect on the over 2,000 solar employees in Washington state. Having the 12th largest solar workforce in the nation, mostly in other sectors of the solar industry, I think we need to be weary of the unintended consequences. Our trade actions could lead to retaliation on our own successful polysilicon industry, for example.

In my home state, REC Silicon has worked very hard to innovate and cut costs and has become the leading low-cost supplier of polysilicon in the world. Trade retaliation from China could endanger roughly 860 American manufacturing jobs that REC Silicon provides, and up to 49,589 jobs nationally.by 2014, according to a recent Brattle Group analysis.

My experience at a technology company taught me that innovation, scale, and American entrepreneurship will always figure out how to drive down costs over the long term. We will win with open markets, and that's why we need to continue pressing for open markets for clean energy rather than imposing new tariffs.

    a. Do you believe that the final result of these recent trade cases will be good for our clean energy industries as a whole?

    b. Do escalating trade complaints on all sides endanger growth, investments, and jobs in emerging clean energy industries?

Question 4. While I am glad to see that the US led the world in private clean energy investment last year, this is just one inning of a long series. I am frankly concerned that we cannot sustain this leadership with the policies we have in place today—even if we extend all of the clean energy tax incentives later this year.

Pew recently profiled the national energy policies by country in its report "Who's Winning the Clean Energy Race." Of the eight key national clean energy policies listed in these country profiles, the US only has three in place—three of the eight—and those include clean energy tax incentives, which we still need to extend, and government procurement, which is increasingly under political attacks. China, in contrast, has six of the key eight national policies in place. And many of our European competitors (including Germany, France, the United Kingdom, and Italy) also have six or more of these critical policies.

This policy gap should be a call to action. We need to continue moving forward, not backward. We need to be working on more aggressive policies to seize this enormous global clean energy market opportunity rather than debating the ones we've already passed on a bipartisan basis.

78

While I have long advocated for bilateral clean energy cooperation with China, I also want to be sure that the United States is the world's leading supplier of clean energy technologies to meet the exploding world demand.

a. In terms of our international competitiveness going forward, what sort of incentives are in place in China to promote clean energy development and deployment and how do they compare to the U.S. from your perspective?
b. Do you believe that if we fail to create the right policies and investment incentives at home, we'll miss out on lucrative opportunities for global leadership in clean energy?
c. Wouldn't placing a clear price on carbon be one of the policies that would spur our clean energy industries?

Question 5. Until the beginning of this Congress, there was an overwhelming consensus that clean energy incentives were a good thing. They worked and created jobs. Just a few years ago, the Cantwell-Ensign bill—which extended many key clean energy credits and established the eight year ITC—passed the Senate by a vote of 93 to 2.

There has been little success this Congress in reaching across the aisle to get these credits extended—or to reform the existing credits to make them more effective. It has been an uphill battle, and certainly not for a lack of trying.

So what's changed? Why are credits which used to enjoy fairly broad support become so partisan? Many of those in Congress who have railed against our attempt to build this new industry have petitioned for clean energy projects for their constituents. And polling from Yale and George Mason University show that they oppose the majority of Americans who want to develop clean energy and invest in research.

So how do we get back on track? As many of you know we have already lost a lot of ground. Many important energy credits have already expired. Or in the case of wind, effectively expired given the placed-in-service requirement. In the short term, I believe that we must extend these credits to maintain the American clean energy jobs that they support.

a. Assuming comprehensive tax reform is not happening this year, will jobs be lost if we fail to extend these expiring credits that industries have been banking on?
b. On the flip side, will businesses create jobs if these provisions are extended for a predictable period of time?
a. As Congress begins to grapple with a major reform of the tax code, would
c. you be willing to trade the certainty of multiyear extensions for a sunset date for all energy tax subsidies?
d. Do you think it's fair that some energy sources benefit from permanent subsidies and others have to deal with the uncertainty of short-term extensions?

Question 6. I want to ask about the scale of advanced energy R&D investment that we need. As you are surely well aware, the energy sector itself invests a far smaller fraction of its revenue in research and new technology development than many other sectors of the American economy. According to one analysis from the Breakthrough Institute, the energy sector invests just two tenths of one percent of annual revenues in R&D, an order of magnitude lower than the national average across all industries (2.6%) and two orders of magnitude lower than leading innovation-driven industries such as biotech, semiconductors or information technology.

The health care sector invests a full 20% of its revenues in R&D and the federal government adds to this with over $30 billion annually in health care research spending through the National Institutes of Health (NIH). Yet despite the far lower levels of private sector energy research spending, the federal government invests just a few billion annually in energy R&D, mostly through the Department of Energy (DOE).

With private sector investment levels like these, there seems to be a strong need for public investments that can fill the gap and help drive the innovation and advanced energy technologies we need. While we certainly have to make some difficult choices when it comes to getting our fiscal house in order, I do not believe critical investments in R&D are the path to a brighter fiscal and economic future. If securing our energy independence, averting climate change and creating new energy industries and jobs are true national priorities, shouldn't our energy R&D budgets be more on the scale of NIH?

Question 7. Biomass is one clean energy sector in which the United States is second to none. We account for roughly 23 percent of the world's installed capacity, compared to China's 7 percent share.

I do not believe this is a coincidence. The long-term market signal that the Renewable Fuel Standard (RFS) sends reduces the uncertainty and unleashes investment. This is precisely what is needed in other sectors—a long term signal that unleashes investment in clean energy.

I am proud that my state is at the forefront of figuring out alternative ways to produce jet fuel from a variety of non-petroleum domestic sources. A broad coalition of researchers, farmers, entrepreneurs, fuel producers, jet makers, airports, and others are all working together to figure out the best way to make green jet fuel. They believe that homegrown jet fuel alternatives will mean real economic growth in Washington state and can create jobs around the nation. They know that instead of sending billions overseas each year for foreign oil, we should be figuring out ways we can keep that money here at home, supporting our economy and workers.

The U.S. military is also leading the way on this opportunity. The U.S. Air Force is currently testing different blends of biofuels and jet fuels, and hopes to acquire 50 percent of its domestic aviation fuel from alternative fuel blends by 2016. The Air Force is the nation's largest user of energy, spending about $8 billion on fuel and electricity every year—about 84 percent of that goes to fuel our aircraft.

The U.S. Navy is also moving forward on biofuels. In an article in the Washington Post, Secretary of the Navy Ray Mabus said that, "[t]he main reason we're moving toward alternative fuels in the Navy and the Marine Corps is to make us better war fighters." Secretary Mabus went on to say that having a Marine either wounded or killed for every 50 convoys of fuel brought into Afghanistan is "just too high a price to pay."

a. Do you believe that the Department of Defense can play an important role in facilitating our emerging domestic biofuels industry?

b. Would these efforts advance our national security, both by decreasing our energy dependence and by reducing our military's expenditures on the full costs of energy over the long term?

○

www.ingramcontent.com/pod-product-compliance
Lightning Source LLC
Chambersburg PA
CBHW081215170526
45165CB00009B/2830